cuisine niçoise

cuisine Niçoise

sun-kissed cooking from the French Riviera

HILLARY DAVIS

photographs by Steven Rothfeld

GIBBS SMITH
TO ENRICH AND INSPIRE HUMANKIND

First Edition
17 16 15 14 13   5 4 3 2 1

Text © 2013 by Hillary Davis
Photographs © 2013 by Steven Rothfeld
Illustrations Shutterstock/Zoom Team

Published by
Gibbs Smith
P.O. Box 667
Layton, Utah 84041

1.800.835.4993 orders
www.gibbs-smith.com

Designed by Sheryl Dickert
Page production by Melissa Dymock
Printed and bound in Hong Kong

Gibbs Smith books are printed on paper produced from sustainable PEFC-certified forest/controlled wood source. Learn more at www.pefc.org.

Library of Congress Cataloging-in-Publication Data

Davis, Hillary.
  Cuisine niçoise : sun-kissed cooking from the French Riviera / Hillary Davis ; photographs by Steven Rothfeld. — First edition.
      pages cm
  Includes index.
  ISBN 978-1-4236-3294-8
  1. Cooking, French. 2. Cooking—France—Nice. I. Rothfeld, Steven, photographer. II. Title.
  TX719.D285 2013
  641.5944—dc23
                    2013002965

Contents

beginnings
Les Entrées

SOUPS
Les Soupes

continued >

salads
Les Salades

pastas, risotto, pizzas
Les Pâtes, Les Risottos, Les Pizzas

vegetables

Les Légumes

continued >

easy weeknights
Les Dîners en Semaine

sunday suppers
Les Dîners de Dimanche

sweet endings
Les Desserts

Introduction

Why had I never heard of cuisine Niçoise?

Why had I never heard of *socca*, or *la trouchia*, *tout-nus* or *tourte de blettes*?

By the time I moved to France, to the village of Bar-sur-Loup in the nearby hills behind Nice, I had spent years cooking my way through dozens and dozens of French cookbooks, learning the styles of cooking—from Normandy, Alsace, Provence, the Basque country, Bordeaux and Lyon. I had lived in Paris. I had vacationed every year in France. I had eaten my way through the French Michelin stars. Yet I had never come across the term *cuisine Niçoise*.

It wasn't until I moved to my village, dined with neighbors, and took food-shopping excursions to Nice that it became clear I had missed something very big. I discovered a way of cooking that was so much more than Salade Niçoise. It was not only a cuisine but also a way of life defined by the sea, the garden, the sun, and the proximity of this corner of France to Italy.

My wonder at finding something so intriguing soon grew into a quest to learn this unsung cuisine, to see if it was worth singing. It all began when we decided to move to the South of France and started looking for a village to call home. I will never forget seeing it for the first time. At a turn in the road, a medieval honey-colored stone village with a chateau appeared at the very top of a hill, high above the surrounding countryside. A sign indicated it was the village of Bar-sur-Loup. We drove up the winding, steep road and got out to walk.

I was home. I could feel it. It was that simple.

This was where I would eventually learn to cook cuisine Niçoise. This was where I would learn to forage, till a garden, harvest olives, buy fresh every day from the local farmers and in the open-air markets, spend my Sundays cooking and sharing meals with friends, and buy locally made pottery to serve it on and locally made wine to serve with it.

BAR-SUR-LOUP

Bar-sur-Loup is in the *pays Niçois*, that area around Nice where they cook "in the style of Nice." The area extends from Grasse, all the way across to Sospel, and from Cannes to Nice and over to Menton. The coastal portion is the Côte d'Azur.

Bar-sur-Loup, a small, perched town with cobblestone alleys, an ancient parish church and panoramic views, is known as the "city of oranges." It holds an annual orange festival, the *Fête de l'Oranger*, because the orange tree loves our village. The *bigarade*, or bitter orange, grows with abandon all over the wide, grassy terraces cut into the steep hills that climb up to the village. As the day warms, they bask in the Mediterranean sun, perfuming the air.

Rosemary grows like a weed all over the countryside. So do tangles of uncultivated roses, fertile fig trees, olive trees, rambling grape vines, and fragrant mimosa trees hanging heavy with bright yellow flowers. Wild lavender and thyme cover the scrubby hills; wild mushrooms sprout in the forests in the fall; and tiny violets intermingle with new grass and wildflowers in the open fields. Herbs blossom madly along paths, at the sides of mountain roads, and in the crooks and crannies of ancient stone walls.

Fruit trees, including bigarade orange, lemon, cherry, olive, and fig, surrounded the house we bought just below the village. Set on four acres, with ancient terraces holding gnarly vines, stone fences, and untamed bushes, the house had a breathtaking view of the dramatic limestone cliffs of the Gorges du Loup, the waterfall cascading down into the canyon of the Gorges, and the even more highly perched village of Gourdon, which in the black night sky seemed to hover like a well-lit flying saucer above our village.

I learned over time that the orange trees around my house bore the fruit that I bought candied in the open-air markets; that their blossoms would go into making the fragrances being produced a few miles away in Grasse, where they extracted essential oil from the flowers and called it "neroli"; that the dried peel is used in bouquet garni; and that its oil is used to flavor France's most famous orange liqueurs, Cointreau and Grand Marnier. A new friend in the next village also informed me one day that the bigarade orange provides the top notes for Miss Dior Cherie perfume!

Those orange trees, that house, the village, and the wild boar that were frequently herded down the road just outside my gate colored my life and changed it forever.

CUISINE NIÇOISE

Cuisine Niçoise is the style of cooking found in Nice, in the countryside around Nice, and for the most part in our village. It comes from humble origins, with most of the recipes having been inherited from grandmothers who prepared farmhouse cuisine from produce grown in their kitchen gardens using recipes that were handed down for generations—and often served to three of them sitting at the kitchen table for Sunday dinner.

Many of those grandmothers were either Italian or French influenced by Italian cuisine, because the entire area along the coast from Cannes towards Monaco had been part of Italy until 1860, when it was ceded to France. So the cuisines of those two countries are entwined and intermingled in the most ideal culinary match of Italian and French traditions. The resulting cuisine Niçoise springs from that marriage—with a strong dash of its own unique dishes not found anywhere else in France.

This area of France fits snugly close to Genoa, so subtle changes were made to typically Italian dishes on a daily basis, thereby creating the evolution of a new blend of French and Italian cooking. French Niçoise cooks make gnocchi, but they fold in chopped Swiss chard; they make ravioli but stuff it with orange-scented beef stew or fry it. A favorite meal of pizza at a restaurant for lunch might be followed by a stew at home for dinner, made with an inexpensive cut of meat that has been marinated overnight in wine. The meat is enhanced with vegetables from the garden at the back of the house and herbs harvested wild from the side of the road during an afternoon walk. The *daube*, or French stew, is most likely served with homemade Italian tagliatelle.

Cuisine Niçoise is as unique a way of cooking as that of Lyon or Alsace; however, you can find the cooking of Lyon and Alsace in restaurants throughout France, whereas much of cuisine Niçoise is found only in the region around Nice. It would be hard to find *socca*, a traditional Niçoise pancake or crêpe made of chickpea flour, once you leave Nice.

Niçoise cooking is vibrant and healthy, with an emphasis on vegetables and fish. It is honest, simple and frugal, based on what is available from the surrounding land and the sea. It is designed with olive oil rather than butter and cream; it is light rather than bathed in rich sauces. Because there is little room for cattle to roam in this region, there is less beef and more lamb, pork, rabbit, wild game, duck and chicken. And cuisine Niçoise depends on fresh, locally sourced produce, either wild or tamed by farmers. You can't speak about it without mentioning the local farmer or fisherman.

In the open-air market in Nice and in small family shops in the area, you will find wild asparagus; wild mushrooms; mesclun; zucchini flowers; *Mara des Bois*—tiny strawberries; red, green, and black fresh figs; fresh green walnuts; lamb from the nearby Alpes-de-Haute Provence; and lean sheep and goat cheeses as well as a vast array of brilliantly colored fruits and vegetables. As much as imaginable, everything at the market is local.

The olive oil that dressed my salads was from the old stone press in Opio, a village down the hill; like my neighbors, I scooped up the olives beneath my trees and drove them down to the olive mill in exchange for a bottle of oil. Bread came from the village baker. Our house wine, Belette rosé, came from the hills behind Nice. Our salad bowl in the summer was filled from my garden and in the winter still filled from my garden but with sturdier varieties of greens. Much of the fish I bought was line caught from local waters, and the cheese that I coveted was from shepherd farmers who descended from the mountains behind Nice to bring their small quantities of handcrafted cheeses to our markets. Neighboring beekeepers, as well, stocked us with golden goodness from the hives in their gardens.

The countryside around Nice is ideal for growing, as the temperature rarely reaches beyond the typical 68- to 86-degree Fahrenheit range. In the hills behind Nice and the Côte d'Azur, in the *arrière-pays*, or backcountry, many sunny microclimates exist, providing superb growing conditions for various types of produce. Bar-sur-Loup's is perfect for growing oranges, while Menton's, down the coast, is ideal for lemons. A drive through the *arrière-pays* yields a delightful variety of culinary treats and specialties. You could begin in Grasse, which is not as conducive to growing food as it is to growing roses, tuberoses, jasmine, gardenias, and honeysuckle; but a couple of miles farther is Opio, where the climate is ideal for olive trees. A short drive east brings you to Bar-sur-Loup, where you experience the microclimate so heavenly for oranges. Farther along, violets thrive in the fields of Tourettes-sur-Loup. Grapes, apricots, and herbs rejoice in the alpine climate of Saint-Jeannet. And the hills surrounding Nice are conducive to cultivating amazing tomatoes and grapes.

As time went on, I became an expert on where to find the best produce, which were the best open-air markets, where to find the best bread, fish, cheese, and honey. The map in my mind soon became populated with croissants, markets, cheese shops, and *confiture* (jam) makers rather than highways and street signs. Everything revolved around food for me, even the geography: hilltop villages were marked on my mind's map with jam and honey shops, while the larger towns were represented by vast open-air markets. The map was decorated with olive branches and colorful fields of lavender.

Soon after moving to Bar-sur-Loup, I yearned to learn what to do with all the produce I found in the markets and shops. Luckily, I found guardian angels of the culinary sort living in and around my village, who taught me traditional cuisine Niçoise that they had learned from their mothers and friends and grandmothers. I took their tutoring seriously, mastered their authentic Niçoise dishes, then updated them for my taste and streamlined them for my busy life. I also tried to find cookbooks to learn cuisine Niçoise and only found one at the time, which had been published in 1972 by the ex-mayor of Nice, Jacques Médecin. This became my bible. Médecin, my neighbors, and friendly local chefs became my guides and mentors. The younger up-and-coming chefs continue to be my inspiration, always using ingredients that are local and fresh, exulting in the possibilities of what can be done with them. Their style of cooking is more modern but always within the way of living and cooking so beloved in this region.

At home, cuisine Niçoise is casual, served on mismatched pottery rather than fine china. It has the cozy familiarity of a grandmother's kitchen, where food was prepared in well-loved vintage pots and served on a long wooden table. Although its allure is a nostalgic one, it fits very much into our times and lifestyles. Simple and homey, using local ingredients or what you have on hand, cuisine Niçoise is an inexpensive and healthy way of cooking that I am thrilled to share with you—because I learned that this unsung cuisine is indeed worth singing.

Niçoise Ingredients

Niçoise cuisine is different from the rest of French cuisine due to the fact that its history and location are unique. Having been part of the Kingdom of Sardinia until 1860, its culinary heritage is just as much Italian as it is French.

As the capital of the southern area of the Alpes called the Alpes-Maritimes, Nice and its style of cooking reigns over the entire area along the French Riviera (or Côte d'Azur) from Cannes all the way to Menton and up to include the hill towns just below the mountains that plunge right down to the Mediterranean sea.

These are the ingredients used most in Niçoise cuisine—the key being to use the very highest quality ingredients you can find. If you have these ingredients on hand, you can easily create the flavors, smells, and pleasures of the cooking from this sun-kissed corner of France.

ANCHOVIES

You would be surprised at how many recipes in this book use anchovies, because in Niçoise cooking they are used to add a subtle salty flavor that you can't quite identify, as well as a pungent one. Niçoise chefs would recommend using salt-cured anchovies, but if you can't find them, use flat or rolled canned ones. If you buy salt-cured anchovies, hold them under running water to clean off the salt, fillet them, and then pat them dry. Anchovy paste is my secret ingredient in many dishes and is an essential item in my pantry.

Marinated fresh anchovies have a silvery color and are sold in gourmet stores. They look and taste quite different from canned anchovies, having a firmer texture and less salt. They make a good topping for pizza and *tartines* and add interest in dips or chopped into sauces and salad dressings.

ARTICHOKES

Small, purple-tipped artichokes grow easily around Nice and are served raw in salads, marinated, or stuffed. For the recipes in this book, use any fresh artichokes available locally. Otherwise, use canned quartered artichokes or artichoke hearts.

BASIL

The intoxicating aroma of fresh basil and garlic being pounded in a mortar and pestle or puréed in a food processor reflects the uplifting quality of a well-made *pistou* — one where plenty of fresh basil leaves are the star ingredients. *Pistou*, the vibrant green paste made with basil, garlic, olive oil, and Parmesan, is dropped into soups, blended into vinaigrettes, painted over fish, and tossed into pastas. Over the border in Genoa, where it is called *pesto*, it is ritually pounded in a marble mortar, the ingredients called for being basil, extra virgin olive oil,

pine nuts, salt, Parmigiano-Reggiano and Pecorino. Over time, as the recipe for pesto migrated to Nice, the pine nuts were dropped.

Basil aids digestion, is a natural anti-inflammatory, and is high in antioxidants. Combined with raw garlic's anti-bacterial qualities, pistou can be considered to have positive medicinal effects on the body as well as soul-nourishing ones.

BREADCRUMBS

If it can be stuffed, the Niçoise do it, absolutely deliciously. The essential ingredient for many of their stuffed dishes, as well as a topping for *tians* (shallow casseroles), is freshly made breadcrumbs.

Homemade breadcrumbs are a breeze to make if you have a food processor or blender. Simply take your favorite bread, slice off the crusts, tear the bread into pieces, put it in the food processor or blender, and pulse or blend until you get the consistency you want. I like to stop when I still have some larger tender pieces in the mix. Don't toss day-old bread. Use it to make breadcrumbs, and store them in a plastic bag in the freezer.

CANDIED FRUITS

Candied fruits, *fruits confit*, are very popular along the Côte d'Azur. Local oranges, clementines, lemons, melons, cherries, apricots, and more are preserved in sugar and displayed like jewels in precious settings. They are considered a special treat, given as gifts, offered on holiday tables, and taken home to dice and use in pastries, cakes, and ice cream. When candied fruits are called for, there are fresh candied fruits that you can order online, or you can look in your local health food store for the ones used to make trail mix and dice them at home.

CANNED TUNA

Canned tuna fish in olive oil is a staple on the shelves of most pantries, as it is a required ingredient in traditional Salade Niçoise. Buy the very best quality you can find packed in olive oil from Sicily, Spain, Italy, or Portugal. Always use tuna packed in olive oil, not in water.

CAPERS

Small flower buds from the caper bush that have been preserved in salt and vinegar, capers perk up a dish and add a distinctly salty note. Rinse them well and pat dry before using.

CHEESE

The Niçoise region is not known for its cheeses but rather for loving to use cheese in almost everything. Grated Parmigiano-Reggiano and Emmental are found topping soups, salads, pastas, and main courses. Cheese should always be freshly grated. Pre-grated cheese has little flavor and is a far cry from the original. Buy a large piece; you can keep it wrapped in the refrigerator and then either grate it or use a vegetable peeler to shave off paper-thin slices to garnish salads and pastas as needed.

Fresh goat cheese is the most widely produced cheese in the region and is sold from farms posting signs along village roads, in open-air markets, and in cheese shops. Two other fresh cheeses—*fromage blanc*, a very soft creamy cheese, and *la brousse*, a creamy goat's-milk cheese—are sold in most cheese shops and used in a variety of dishes, both savory and sweet.

CHICKPEAS

Dried chickpeas (garbanzo beans) can be soaked then used in recipes; but for the most part, I use canned chickpeas, which are time-saving and easy. They are excellent in salads, soups, and stews, besides being high in protein and fiber.

CHICKPEA FLOUR

Many Niçoise dishes call for chickpea flour, which is yet another reason why this style of cooking is so healthy. Chickpea flour, made from garbanzo beans, is gluten free and packed with protein. It has a slightly nutty flavor that makes *socca, panisses,* and batters so memorable as being uniquely Niçoise.

FENNEL

Fish markets in the region often add dried fennel stalks to packages of fish so the cook can use it to either stuff the fish or lay it down on a barbeque or baking pan for the fish to cook on. Dried fennel seeds are used in many dishes, warmed in a skillet first to release their aroma. And fresh fennel accents many regional recipes; its feathery fronds are a delightful addition to any chopped herb blend. Fennel's popularity in Niçoise cuisine comes full circle when you consider that the favorite anise-flavored drinks, Pernod and Pastis, have wild fennel as one of their ingredients.

FLOUR

For pastry, pasta, or bread I use organic unbleached all-purpose flour. Chickpea flour is the favorite flour of the Niçoise, turning up in a myriad of dishes from socca to batter. Look for garbanzo (chickpea) flour in gourmet shops, health food stores, and ethnic groceries.

FRESH HERBS

Basil, sage, thyme, flat leaf parsley, marjoram, and rosemary are used extensively. *Réfrescat*, a mix unique to Niçoise cuisine, is made from herbs that are not always easy to locate, including borage, purslane, poppy, dandelion, and sow-thistle; but if you can find the seeds you can grow them at home. Although dried herbs are available in the supermarket, the Niçoise style of cooking traditionally uses only fresh herbs. When a recipe calls for a bouquet garni or herbes de Provence, it means using fresh herbs, not dried.

GARLIC

Always fresh! Garlic is one of the main ingredients used in this style of cooking, for its flavor as well as its health benefits. So much garlic is used that many homes have a large bowl of fresh garlic on the counter near the stove or a whole wreath of it hung in a cool place, ready to use.

LEMONS

Menton, just down the road from Nice, is known for its glorious citrus fruits, which thrive in its protected subtropical microclimate. The famous fat, juicy Menton lemons are in everyone's basket when shopping in open-air markets, so many Niçoise recipes incorporate lemons. Try to buy only organic and non-treated lemons, especially if you are going to use the zest.

LENTILS

The tiny *lentilles de Puy* from the Auvergne region of France are the only lentils I use and the ones you see most often in dishes from this region. I love their taste, texture, and ability to hold their own in any dish. Keeping them on hand means you can easily whip up a quick lentil salad or soup, as they cook very quickly.

MESCLUN

Invented in Nice by farmers above the city who came up with this idea to differentiate their greens from others being sold, mesclun is traditionally meant to be miscellaneous young greens barely dressed with olive oil, lemon juice, and salt. Jacques Médecin, the ex-mayor of Nice who codified a great deal of Niçoise recipes, describes mesclun as being a mixture of baby dandelion leaves, young lettuce, and arugula.

MUSHROOMS

There is a long tradition of foraging for mushrooms in the Niçoise countryside. Most villages, restaurants, and the open-air markets in larger towns are the beneficiaries of an abundance of wild mushrooms brought to them by individuals who have picked them that morning. The most popular are the meaty *cèpes*, or porcini. Use chanterelles, cèpes, portobellos, or morels; otherwise, the lovely white button mushrooms, *champignons de Paris*, found in most markets work well in almost any recipe that calls for mushrooms, cooked or raw.

OLIVES

If you can't find the small purplish-brownish-black Niçoise olives from the *cailletier* olive trees, which are grown in the region around Nice, use oil-cured black olives or even canned pitted black olives, depending on the recipe. Canned pitted black olives can lack in flavor and texture, so making the extra effort to buy whole black olives and pitting them yourself will make a huge flavor difference. Buy and keep jars of Niçoise, Calabrese, Kalamata, and Gaeta olives on your shelf when you find them in specialty or gourmet stores.

OLIVE OIL

Olive oil is to Niçoise cooking what butter is to cooking in northern France. Golden-colored extra virgin Niçoise olive oil is excellent for most cooking as well as for frying, because it makes everything taste better and seems to do fine at high frying temperatures. For everyday cooking, look for an extra virgin olive oil from Spain, Italy, or France from big brand-name companies.

When I want to dress a salad or finish a dish and am looking for a stronger, fruitier flavor, I use either extra virgin Spanish or Sicilian olive oils. I've learned over time to bring home bottles of olive oil from different small olive growers when I travel through Italy and France, as olives take on the characteristics of their terroir, and a variety of oils in the pantry with different flavors makes cooking and dressing salads more fun. These single-estate olive oils, produced in small batches with a great deal of attention to the final taste and quality, are more expensive and rare. Olive oil aficionados are as passionate as wine connoisseurs about their favorite olive growers, harvests, type of olive, year, and terroir. Following their suggestions has led me to many a memorable olive oil.

ORANGES

The *bigarade* orange, which Bar-sur-Loup is famous for, is similar to the Seville orange. Oranges grow so well in the Niçoise countryside that they have become an integral ingredient in many dishes, both savory and sweet.

PASTA

Angel hair, spaghetti, wide egg noodles, and ravioli cradle the sauces born from the marriage of Genovese Italian cuisine and southern French cuisine in this region of France. Having on hand a stock of the best durum flour dried pastas is necessary to prepare many regional dishes. Always cook pasta in plenty of salted boiling water, without oil, allowing at least 4 ounces per person. Drain the pasta, then immediately put it in a skillet or saucepan with the sauce and toss to coat over medium heat for a minute before serving.

Fresh pasta is quicker than ever to make with a food processor. It cooks more quickly than dried pasta and adds a certain tenderness that can truly elevate a dish. It can be made ahead and frozen until ready to use.

PINE NUTS

Do you know where they come from? They are kernels taken from pinecones! So you can imagine why they are expensive—painstaking labor is involved to extract every one. Pine nuts are an essential ingredient in making *tourte de blettes*, *la trouchia*, and other typical dishes and pastries. Buy them in small amounts and keep them in the refrigerator.

POLENTA

You can use any fine cornmeal to make polenta, or look for packages labeled *polenta*. Ideally, organic stone-ground cornmeal would be the best choice.

RAISINS

Raisins are part of the sweet and salty combination that I love so much about Niçoise cuisine. You'll often see raisins in savory dishes, adding that little bite of sweetness that is so intriguing. Containers of both dark and blond raisins are an essential ingredient in a Niçoise pantry.

SALT

I have six salt boxes lined up by my stove. One holds fine sea salt for general cooking; one for coarse French gray salt; one for Malden flaked sea salt, which I love to use as a finishing salt or over sweet butter for crunch; one for Himalayan pink salt; and two boxes for salt blends that I make.

Next to the salt boxes I have three peppercorn boxes for Tellicherry black, pink, and white. I keep a small mortar and pestle nearby and a spice grinder to quickly grind up impromptu blends of coarse salt, peppercorns, and herbs designed for specific dishes. I serve these in individual salt bowls on the table or in a small mound at the end of each plate. Though salt is not unique to Niçoise cooking, it has become an integral part of the way I cook at home.

SARDINES

Fresh sardines are stuffed, sliced, added to the tops of pizzas, rolled and baked, mashed into spreads, and put between slices of bread with a slice of onion. Try to find fresh sardines or ask your fish market to order them for you. They are light little fish with a firm flesh. *Do not use canned sardines;* they're not at all the same.

STOCKFISH

Preserved to the point of being stiff as a board, stockfish is air-dried cod, used to make a Niçoise fish stew called *estocaficada*, with potatoes and olives. I use salt cod as a substitute to save time, and I prefer the lighter flavor.

SWISS CHARD

The queen of Niçoise vegetables, Swiss chard appears in a wide variety of recipes, both sweet and savory. When it is out of season, the Niçoise substitute spinach.

TOMATOES

Luscious plump tomatoes are grown on hillsides, in kitchen gardens, trellised over twig gates, and nurtured in luminous white indoor growing sheds. The rosy glow of a vendor's cheeks in the market comes from trying to keep up with bagging tomatoes for enthusiastic early shoppers. You know where the best are by quickly scanning down the aisles, looking for lines three deep. Tomatoes come in a tantalizing variety: dark green, zebra striped, purple-brown, cherry size, and some with deep swirls of ridges.

ZUCCHINI

The little round zucchini found in the open-air markets are perfect for stuffing Niçoise style. The longer ones are stuffed as well, and the zucchini flowers are stuffed, fried, and used in soups.

Author's Note

The Niçoise style of cooking is casual and homey. There are no hard-and-fast rules as there are in haute cuisine, only the guideline to use the very best of what you have on hand locally. So you should feel free to substitute ingredients or adjust seasoning to your taste for the recipes in this book.

I tested all the recipes in my home kitchen, have prepared many of them for years, and have dozens of friends and volunteers who have tested them as well. Yet, while I have a garden and pick large beefsteak tomatoes, a friend may find small ones in a farmer's market. Using what we have on hand means measurements can vary; so in as many instances as possible I have indicated more precise amounts for these types of ingredients.

Also, using an oven thermometer to be more accurate about baking temperatures is helpful. Even if your oven is new, it can vary from another person's oven. Altitude baking versus low-altitude baking, as well as humidity, will affect recipes; so, again, check during the process of preparing a recipe and read the recipe ahead before beginning to cook.

The Niçoise way of preparing food is all about being present with it and enjoying the experience of working with food: tossing a meatball into the air; getting your hands into the center of a salad and gently massaging it with aromatic oil, savoring the scent; feeling a thrill when your cake rises. Rather than walking away from your food while it cooks, staying with it and waiting for it to respond to you is ultimately satisfying.

This way of cooking can take very little time, or most of a Sunday. Either way, if you become aware of its simple beauty and connection to a people and their culture, as well as the way cooking connects us all, it will nourish your soul.

Beginnings

Les Entrées

SWISS CHARD STEMS STUFFED WITH TUNA
Les Côtes de Blettes Frites, Farcies au Thon

One of the most surprising things about buying a house in France is the lack of a kitchen: most people dismantle theirs so the new owners have the opportunity to install one to their liking. Mine had even had the cabinets ripped out, and a water pipe was dangling from the wall where a sink should have been. Until I could piece together a kitchen, we ate out a lot!

The sun, sand, and shimmering waters that attract millions of vacationers to the Côte d'Azur every year also attract world-class chefs to cater to them. It was an easy drive for us to get down to the coast and dine in the restaurants. Nothing quite compares to dining at a fabulous restaurant at a table set on the sand under the stars. White tablecloths, sparkling wine glasses and cutlery, and samplings of local cuisine made our evenings a huge treat. I would inevitably come away inspired with new ideas.

One night we planned our dinner so that we could enjoy the sun setting over the Mediterranean. I remember that night as much for the appetizer placed before me as for the fuchsia-colored sky. It was a plate of deep-fried Swiss chard stems that had been sandwiched with a filling of Swiss cheese and thinly sliced ham. Served with our wine, it made a wonderful snack before our dinner arrived.

Crispy on the outside, creamy on the inside, this recipe for deep-fried Swiss chard stems is instead stuffed with tuna and has become one of my favorite small bites to offer guests. Fry the Swiss chard leaves separately and serve on the side. They literally disappear on your tongue!

Yields 12-15 pieces, more if stalks are longer

12 Swiss chard stems, with leaves

2 slices white bread, crusts removed

1 (5-ounce) can solid light tuna in olive oil, drained, oil reserved

1½ teaspoons capers, drained

2 eggs

1 cup flour

2 cups vegetable oil

salt

Tear the leaves from the Swiss chard stalks; wash the leaves and pat very dry. Reserve.

Wash and dry the stalks. Slice each stalk into 3-inch pieces. Trim as you would rhubarb or celery, peeling away any tough fibers from the outside of the stalks with a small knife.

Bring a pot of water to a boil, drop the stem pieces in, and cook for 15 minutes, until they are tender. Drain in a colander and pat dry.

Tear the slices of bread and place in a food processor with the tuna, 2 tablespoons of the reserved tuna oil, and capers. Process until smooth.

Beat the eggs in a shallow bowl. Place the flour on a large plate for dredging.

Make sandwiches by spooning generous amounts of the tuna mixture onto a piece of chard, topping it with another piece of chard, and gently pressing the two together all the way around to make secure bundles. Continue until you have all the "sandwiches" made.

Heat the oil in a frying pan to 360 degrees F. Dip the sandwiches into the egg to coat, then roll them in flour and shake off excess. Fry only a few seconds on each side, until golden brown.

Remove to a paper towel and sprinkle with salt. Serve immediately, or keep warm in the oven until all the sandwiches are done.

Keeping the oil at the same temperature, drop in the dry Swiss chard leaves for a few seconds; remove before they brown. Drain on paper towels, sprinkle with a little salt, and then pile like fallen leaves on a plate. Serve beside the Swiss chard sandwiches. Plan on 4 Swiss chard sandwiches per person.

HOUSE OLIVES
Les Olives Chez Nous

It was a rainy day in Antibes and the dry haven of the covered market beckoned me. As I closed my umbrella, I was drawn towards two scrubbed pine tables outside a shop that displayed pottery jars for oil and vinegar and the ubiquitous piles of multicolored perfumed soap you find all over the South of France.

One table also had stacks of odd little plates with short, pointed spikes in the center, which I was told are used for scraping fresh garlic cloves. I also was drawn to a hand-painted dish with two connected bowls for serving olives: you put the olives in one of the bowls and leave the other one empty for the pits. I bought three, remembering that most of the people we knew had offered olives with wine when we would visit. Everyone seemed to have their own blend of house olives with different dressings, so I thought these little bowls would be perfect for serving my three house olive recipes—when I decided what they would be!

As well as in those bowls, I frequently serve olives on a fragrant bed of rosemary or, during the holidays, on an angelic wreath of rosemary arranged on a large round serving platter.

Use the best fruity extra virgin olive oil you can find, and marinate the olives for at least a day in the following three dressings before serving.

Makes 1 - 1 1/2 cups each

BLACK OLIVES WITH ORANGE

Living in the "city of oranges," with an orange tree just outside of my kitchen, it seemed fitting to make an olive blend with oranges and some lemon.

4 tablespoons extra virgin olive oil

4 tablespoons fresh orange juice

1/2 teaspoon salt

4 teaspoons sugar

1 small clove garlic, pressed

4 teaspoons white vinegar

1 tablespoon Cointreau orange liqueur

3 tablespoons finely grated orange rind

1 (6-ounce) can or jar pitted black olives, best quality available

1/2 lemon, rind only, coarsely chopped

Whisk the olive oil, orange juice, salt, sugar, garlic, vinegar, Cointreau and orange rind together. Pour over the olives and toss with a fork to mix. Place everything in a screw-top glass jar and refrigerate to marinate for at least 1 day before serving.

To serve, spoon the olives into a bowl. Strain and reserve the marinade in another bowl to capture the orange rind; spoon rind over the top of the olives, sprinkle the chopped lemon peel over the top as well, and add a little drizzle of the marinade. Discard any remaining marinade.

GREEN OLIVES WITH BLACK OLIVE FENNEL DRESSING

I usually serve Pernod with this olive mix to celebrate the combination of anise and fennel flavors together.

1 clove garlic, sliced in thirds

1/2 cup extra virgin olive oil

3 teaspoons sugar

1 teaspoon fresh lemon juice

2 teaspoons white vinegar

1/4 teaspoon fennel seeds

3 tablespoons chopped fresh fennel frond

8 pitted oil-cured black olives

1 cup pitted green olives, drained

2 tablespoons grated fresh fennel bulb

Place the garlic, olive oil, sugar, lemon juice, vinegar, fennel seeds, and fennel frond in a food processor and blend for 15 seconds. Add the oil-cured olives and pulse until finely chopped.

Place the green olives in a bowl, pour the vinaigrette over the top, and toss with a fork to mix well. Add the grated fennel bulb and mix again. Put everything in a screw-top glass jar or container and refrigerate for at least 1 day before serving.

To serve, spoon the olives into a bowl. Strain the marinade through a sieve, discard the liquid, and spoon the remaining grated fennel, fronds and seeds over the top of the olives before serving.

BLACK OLIVES WITH HOMEMADE HARISSA

I make my own harissa paste — a thick hot and spicy condiment used in sandwiches and added to dishes as any other hot sauce. This recipe will be more than enough to lightly coat the olives and still have plenty left over. It keeps well in the refrigerator, with a small amount of olive oil on top, for at least two weeks.

3 fresh red chilis

1 teaspoon fennel seed

$1/2$ teaspoon coriander seed

1 roasted red pepper in oil

$1/2$ teaspoon ground cumin

1 teaspoon smoked paprika

5 cloves garlic

4 sun-dried tomatoes in oil

$2 1/2$ teaspoons sugar

1 teaspoon salt

1 tablespoon fresh lemon juice

4 tablespoons extra virgin olive oil

1 (6-ounce) can or jar pitted black olives, best quality available

Slice the stems off the chilis, then slice them vertically and add to the bowl of a food processor, including the seeds.

Heat the fennel and coriander seeds in a skillet over medium heat just until you can smell their aroma. Remove from the heat and add to the food processor.

Dry the roasted red pepper in a paper towel and add to the food processor. Add the cumin, paprika, garlic, sun-dried tomatoes, sugar, salt, lemon juice, and olive oil; pulse, then process until it is the consistency of tomato paste.

Put the olives in a bowl, spoon the harissa over them, and toss with a fork to coat. Place inside a screw-top glass jar or container and refrigerate at least 1 day before serving.

To serve, spoon out the olives into a serving bowl with a light coating of the harissa, as it is quite spicy and hot. Keep the rest of the harissa refrigerated in a screw-top jar.

TORN SOCCA WITH SEA SALT AND BLACK PEPPER
La Socca

Early on, I decided that one of the ways to learn cuisine Niçoise was to eat my way through Nice's many restaurants. One of those restaurants was more like a snack stop. On market days I would walk there through the narrow, winding streets of old town, where houses are painted the colors of fruits and vegetables—avocado green, deep cranberry, lemon yellow, apricot, and melon—highlighted by shafts of light filtering down from above.

At Specialities Niçoise Socca, I discovered *socca*—the most delicious, uncomplicated chickpea crêpe. It underlined for me what this style of cooking is about. *Socca* is nutritious, healthy, and heart-warming, made with humble ingredients. Rarely found outside of Nice or the Nice countryside, it is a simple pleasure that brings people together under the Mediterranean sun to stand in line for their paper plate, to pick up the torn pieces of socca with their fingers, and to savor the dish that is so emblematic of the Niçoise way of life.

Socca is made from a batter of chickpea flour, water, and olive oil and cooked on huge, searing-hot flat pans into very thin crêpes. The cook uses a paddle to even out the batter in a large circle, then bakes it in a wood-burning oven until the underside is crisp.

The trick to making it at home is to get the oven really hot and heat the pan in the oven long enough so the batter sizzles when you pour it in. Many recipes for socca call for baking it on very high heat, but I find that putting it directly under the broiler after it is baked works best—a tip I learned from a recipe by Mark Bittman. This produces a crispy crêpe with slightly charred edges. It's as close to the real thing as you can get. Socca should be eaten while it is hot, so pass it around immediately. If you fall in love with socca, as I have, and you visit Nice, you can buy your own copper socca pan to make it in.

Serves 4

1 cup chickpea flour

2 tablespoons extra virgin olive oil, plus more for oiling skillet or pan

1 teaspoon salt

1 cup water

1/4 teaspoon turmeric

fine sea salt

freshly ground black pepper

Mix together all ingredients and let stand for 1/2 hour. The batter should be the consistency of thick cream, so whisk in a little more water if needed to thin.

Preheat oven to 475 degrees F. Generously oil a large ovenproof skillet, cast-iron crêpe pan, or baking pan with olive oil and place in the oven for 15 minutes to heat. Swirl some batter in the hot pan to just coat; place in the oven to bake for about 10 minutes. Then remove the pan from the oven while you heat the broiler.

Turn off the oven and turn on the broiler. When it is ready, place the socca under the broiler for about 2 to 3 minutes, until golden brown and crispy, then turn the socca crêpe over and allow the other side to turn golden and crispy. Remove from oven. Slice into uneven shards and present on paper napkins or on a large platter with a generous sprinkling of salt and lots of freshly ground black pepper. Repeat process until the remaining batter is used.

CHICKPEA FLOUR

Chickpea flour is made from dried garbanzo beans. It is used extensively in Niçoise cuisine, most notably in *socca, panisses* (chickpea fries), and as a batter for frying. In Genoa, just down the coast from Nice, chickpea flour is used for making *farinata,* a flatbread.

Chickpea flour is a wonderfully nutritious ingredient to work with. It is gluten-free and compared to wheat flour is high in protein, fiber, and iron. One cup of chickpea flour has 10 grams of dietary fiber and 21 grams of protein, plus good amounts of phosphorous, calcium, iron, folate, and manganese.

You can find chickpea (garbanzo) flour at most health food and gourmet food stores, and you can order it online at www.bobsredmill.com.

FRESH HERB CHEESE WITH HONEY AND TOAST
Le Fromage Frais aux Fines Herbes et au Miel, Pain Grillé

Just days after moving into my house below the village, my neighbors up the hill paid a visit. Monsieur and Madame of an older age arrived bearing a gift—a rustic plum tart Madame had just baked. As they were leaving, she invited me to come see her the next day.

A cool, damp mist was falling as I walked up the steep hill to her house. We sat in her warm kitchen on rush-seated chairs at a small, square wooden table and got to know each other over toasts she had made with a baguette from the village baker, a bit of floral honey, and some fresh cheese. Just before she served the toasts, she finely chopped herbs and edible flowers from her garden and showered them on top. Monsieur joined us only long enough to pour us small glasses of his homemade orange wine.

As I was leaving, Madame gave me a baguette and a wooden spoon. It was her way of answering my question of whether she would be willing to teach me how to cook her family recipes.

The hot Mediterranean sun was shining again and the sky was a brilliant blue as I headed back down the hill. I could smell the earth warming as I walked and could see my sun-drenched terrace below and the fruit trees surrounding my house. I smiled. My new life was starting with a baguette and a wooden spoon. *Perfect!*

A good *fromage frais* (fresh cheese) can be hard to find outside of France, so substitute the following easy-to-make fresh yogurt cheese for a wonderful treat, and remember to make it the night before you want to serve it.

Serves 8

16	ounces plain yogurt
	fine sea salt
8	slices country-style bread, toasted
1/2	cup honey
	any amount of fresh herbs, finely chopped
	Optional: edible flowers, minced dried fruits, or minced garlic and chives

To make the fresh cheese, fit a colander inside a large pot and line the colander with three layers of cheesecloth, allowing some to hang over the sides. Scoop the yogurt on top of the cheesecloth and fold the cheesecloth over the yogurt. I usually twist the cheesecloth and tie it with a knot. Cover with plastic wrap and a lid; refrigerate overnight or for up to 24 hours.

Spoon the yogurt cheese out of the colander and into a bowl. Add salt to taste.

To serve, scoop a generous portion of fresh cheese on top of the toasts, drizzle with honey, then shower with finely chopped herbs.

FRIED SALT COD BALLS
Les Accras

I especially love to snack on the weightless morsels called *accras* that are sold at Specialities Niçoise Socca. The soft, round balls of salt cod fried in a yeast batter until golden brown are presented on a paper plate with wedges of lemon.

To simplify making them at home, I eliminate the yeast and use baking powder. After soaking the salt cod for two days and changing the water at least three times a day, the recipe goes very quickly.

Using extra virgin olive oil for frying enhances their flavor.

Serves 4, makes about 25-30

1 pound salt cod

1 cup all-purpose flour

$1/2$ teaspoon baking powder

$1/2$ cup milk

1 egg

3 cloves garlic, pressed

3 tablespoons finely minced chives

   pinch of cayenne pepper

3 cracks of freshly ground black pepper

   extra virgin olive oil for frying

   lemon wedges for garnish

   fine sea salt

Thoroughly rinse the salt cod and slice it into 2-inch pieces. Immerse them in a bowl of water, cover with plastic wrap, and refrigerate for 2 days. During this time, change the water frequently to eliminate salt.

Drain the cod in a colander, then rinse well again under running water. Place on paper towels to drain, and squeeze well to press out all the water. Carefully feel the cod with your fingers and pull out any bones or skin.

Drop the cod into boiling water and cook for 2 minutes. Drain and squeeze very dry.

Chop the cod finely or pulse it in a food processor; then place in a bowl.

Whisk together the flour and baking powder; add to the bowl of codfish and mix with a fork.

Whisk together the milk, egg, garlic, chives, cayenne, and pepper; then add to the bowl. Mix well.

Heat olive oil to 360 degrees F. in a skillet, deep enough to reach halfway up the balls. Drop the batter by the tablespoon, about the size of a quarter, into the hot oil and fry a few at a time until they are brown on all sides, about 3 minutes. Drain on paper towels, sprinkle with salt, and serve immediately with wedges of lemon.

CHILLED MUSSELS
WITH TARRAGON SHALLOT MAYONNAISE
Les Moules Glacées à la Mayonnaise d'Estragon et d'Échalote

The first time I saw the priest, he was standing alone by the door of the church, his long black cassock tugged by the wind. He stood waiting, then disappeared inside. I later found out there was mass here every day. It made me happy, because it seemed sad when I entered the church to always find it so dark. Most of the time the doors were locked, and when they were open I had to insert a coin in a metal slot and crank a small knob in order to illuminate the church lights. When I did, there was just enough time to make a quick walk around and get back to the front door before being plunged into darkness again. The church even smelled empty.

The next time I saw him was in the café located inside the chateau in the village. He was seated at a table, with one hand on a devotional book and the other raising a mussel shell up towards his mouth. *Père Qui Mange,* I heard the café owner affectionately call him: Father Who Eats.

"He always orders the same thing. We make it for him in the restaurant kitchen and bring it out to him here in the café. Would you like to have some? Come back tomorrow lunchtime and I will have a plate ready for you."

This was what I was learning was so typical of our village—in fact, of the entire surrounding countryside. Food and sharing in its enjoyment were a normal part of life. Of course I would come back the next day!

I ordered a carafe of wine and waited. My mussels arrived. They were delectable. Père Qui Mange knew a good thing when he ate it.

Serves 4

2 pounds fresh mussels

2 cups dry white wine or water

2 egg yolks, room temperature

1/2 cup vegetable oil

1/2 cup extra virgin olive oil

2 1/2 teaspoons white wine vinegar or white balsamic vinegar

2 teaspoons fresh lemon juice

1/2 teaspoon Dijon mustard

1/2 teaspoon fine sea salt

1 1/2 teaspoons sugar

1 small shallot, minced

1/2 tablespoon minced fresh tarragon leaves

Under running water, clean each mussel individually. Pull off the beard, check to see that each mussel is firmly closed, and discard any that are open. Place the mussels in a colander and spray with water to give a final cleaning. (*Tip:* de-bearding mussels kills them instantly, so make sure to cook yours right away.)

Place the cleaned mussels in a large pot on the stove and add the white wine or water. Cover with a lid and cook on high heat until the mussels have opened. Remove from the stove, discard any that have not opened, and cool in the refrigerator.

Place the egg yolks in the bowl of a stand mixer and beat until pale yellow and thick, about 1 minute. Slowly drip in the two oils, drop by drop at first, and keep beating until you achieve the consistency of mayonnaise.

In a small bowl, whisk together the vinegar, lemon juice, mustard, salt, sugar, shallot, and tarragon; then pour the vinegar mixture into the mayonnaise and briefly beat to blend. Taste for seasoning and adjust; thin with a bit of water if needed.

To serve, pull the top shells off the mussels and leave the mussels resting in their bottom shells. Arrange on four plates. Spoon a small dollop of mayonnaise on top of each mussel.

NICOLAS RONDELLI'S FRIVOLITIES
Les Frivolités de L'Hostellerie du Château

The café in the historic chateau is gone now, and a hotel has opened there, with its own Michelin one-star restaurant, Le Bigaradier. The chef, Nicolas Rondelli, is a young, enthusiastic, born and bred Niçoise, treasuring his background while helping it evolve to the next level. His dining room has a stunning view over the Loup Valley towards the coast, and his kitchen is large, modern, and pristine. I can't wait to see how he develops in this just about perfect environment.

I am so happy to include an amuse-bouche recipe for Nicolas's fresh focaccia bread with four toppings. Make the toppings a day ahead for maximum flavor, and serve the day you bake the bread. Slice the bread into bite-size squares or rectangles and present beside the toppings.

EGGPLANT CAVIAR

Makes about 2 cups

1   large eggplant

3   cloves garlic, sliced into thin matchsticks, plus 1 clove minced

5   tablespoons extra virgin olive oil, divided

2   teaspoons fine sea salt

$1/2$ teaspoon black pepper

6   large fresh basil leaves, minced

4   fresh marjoram leaves, minced

    fleur de sel

Heat the oven to 300 degrees F. Lay a sheet of foil on a baking pan.

Slice the eggplant in half lengthwise, make crisscross slashes with the point of a knife, slip matchsticks of garlic into the slices, and season all over with 4 tablespoons of the olive oil, and the salt and pepper. Place the eggplant face down on the baking pan, and cover with a piece of foil. Gently crimp the top and bottom foils together around the edges to make a packet. Bake for 1 hour and check. The eggplant should be very soft. If not, bake another 30 to 60 minutes, until soft. The baking time depends on the size of the eggplant.

Remove from the oven, uncover, and place in a colander to drain off liquid and cool.

Scoop out the pulp and discard the skin. Finely chop the eggplant pulp, and mix in remaining tablespoon olive oil, minced garlic, basil, and marjoram. Taste and adjust salt and pepper if needed, then spoon into a serving bowl and sprinkle with a little fleur de sel.

MARINATED RED PEPPERS

Makes about 1 1/2 cups

3   medium red bell peppers

3   tablespoons extra virgin olive oil, divided

1   teaspoon salt

2   cloves garlic, minced, divided

1   teaspoon fleur de sel

    freshly ground black pepper

Heat the oven to 400 degrees F. Lay a piece of foil on a baking pan and lightly brush with oil.

Slice the tops off the peppers, cut in half vertically, and remove the seeds. Coat peppers with 2 tablespoons oil, sprinkle with salt and half of the minced garlic, and bake for 40 minutes. Remove from the oven, cover with plastic wrap or foil, and let sit for 15 minutes. Remove the wrap and let sit uncovered for 5 minutes.

Peel the skins off the peppers and discard. Slice peppers into thin pieces, then place in a serving bowl with 1 tablespoon olive oil, fleur de sel, pepper to taste, and the remaining garlic. Mix well and taste for seasonings.

continued >

ONION CONFIT

Makes about 1 1/2 cups

- 3 tablespoons extra virgin olive oil
- 2 medium white onions, finely minced
- 2 teaspoons minced fresh rosemary
- 1 teaspoon salt
- 1/4 teaspoon black pepper

Heat the olive oil in a skillet. Place the onions in the skillet with the rosemary, salt, and pepper, and cook over medium-low heat until onions are lightly colored and soft, about 30 minutes. Taste and adjust seasonings, then spoon into a serving bowl.

TAPENADE

Makes about 1 cup

- 10 anchovies in oil
- 2 tablespoons capers
- 3 cloves garlic
- 4 large basil leaves

   extra virgin olive oil
- 1 can or jar pitted black olives, best quality available

In a food processor or mortar and pestle, blend the anchovies, capers, garlic, and basil leaves. Add olive oil in a thin stream until you have a spreadable paste.

Coarsely chop or slice the olives. Mix with the smooth paste and spoon into a serving bowl.

OLIVE OIL FOCACCIA

$^1/_2$ cup olive oil, divided

$1^2/_3$ cups warm water, plus more if needed

1 package active dry yeast (2 $^1/_4$ teaspoons)

$4^1/_2$ cups all-purpose flour

3 teaspoons fine sea salt

extra virgin olive oil to drizzle

fleur de sel

Oil an 11 x 17-inch shallow baking pan with $^1/_4$ cup olive oil.

Pour the water into the bowl of a stand mixer and sprinkle the yeast on top. Allow to sit for 8 minutes. Add remaining $^1/_4$ cup olive oil, flour, and salt; mix with a dough hook until blended. Dribble in more water, if needed, until the dough forms a ball. You want a wet and sticky dough, but one that is formed and elastic to the touch. (Note: if you are doing this by hand, place the water and yeast in a small bowl and allow to rest for 8 minutes. Place the flour and salt in a large bowl, make a well in the center, pour in the water with the yeast and the olive oil, and mix well, first with a wooden spoon and then with your hands. Bring the dough together into a ball, adding drips of water if needed to bring it together.)

Cover the bowl with a towel and let rise until double in size, about $1^1/_2$ to 2 hours.

Punch the dough down, then with oiled or floured hands scoop it out of the bowl onto a clean floured work surface and knead for about 3 minutes, until smooth and elastic.

Place the dough on the oiled baking pan and press outward with your fingers until it fits the entire pan. Gently indent the dough with a finger every few inches.

Cover with plastic wrap, set in a warm place, and allow to rise again for about 45 minutes.

Preheat the oven to 425 degrees F.

Put the focaccia in the oven and bake until it is golden brown, about 30 minutes.

Remove from the oven, drizzle with olive oil and sprinkle with fleur de sel, then cool for 5 minutes. Slice into uniform rectangles, about 1 x 2 inches.

Le Bigaradier Restaurant
L'Hostellerie du Château
6–8, Place Francis Paulet
06620 Bar-sur-Loup
Telephone: (33) 04 93 42 41 10
www.lhostellerieduchateau.com

LE BAR-SUR-LOUP

The village of Bar-sur-Loup is in a setting right out of a movie. It is perched high above the valley, with huge cliffs and cascading waterfalls behind it, with the perched village of Gourdon hovering still higher. It even has a chateau.

A walk in the village square offers amazing views and an exploration of its narrow streets a peek into what life must have been like when this village was a Roman fortress town. If you walk to the side of the church, a Roman tombstone is embedded in the wall beside the door. The fifteenth-century church, L'Eglise de Saint-Jacques-le-Majeur, houses an altarpiece painted by Ludovico Brea and a very old anonymous Niçoise painting of note called *Danse Macabre*, which draws the interest of art historians because it is extremely unusual.

It seemed an omen that we were meant to live there when I discovered that Bar-sur-Loup has a special relationship with America: Admiral de Grasse, an American Revolutionary War hero who fought off the British fleet at Chesapeake Bay and led the victory of Yorktown, was born in the chateau. There is a monument in his honor at Riverwalk Landing in Yorktown, and there is also a statue of him in the village square.

Today, Le Bar-sur-Loup is a mecca for hikers and paragliders. It is known as the city of oranges, with its vin d'orange and orange marmalade specialties being sold every year on Easter Monday at the Fête de L'Oranger.

ASPARAGUS WITH SOFT-BOILED EGG DIP
Les Asperges avec Oeufs à la Coquee

A tender asparagus spear was advanced toward my waiting mouth. We were sitting across from each other at a table in the dappled shade of a restaurant garden, and my newly found English friend, Pamela, was raving about the dish in front of her. It was a plate holding a soft-boiled egg and a pile of asparagus. She had squeezed a lemon over the asparagus before dipping it into the soft egg yolk, and then offered it to me to taste.

It was like instant hollandaise sauce—brilliant! And so simple that I folded it into my memory, inspired to make a version at home. The dish was served on a buttery yellow faience plate, as luminous and beautiful as the sunshine around us. I made plans with my friend to go on a treasure hunt for tableware made of faience on our next outing. How wonderful it would be to have plates that resembled the sun!

Serves 4

16 spears asparagus, cleaned

4 large eggs, room temperature

1 teaspoon fresh lemon juice, divided

fine sea salt

freshly ground white pepper

½ lemon

4 egg cups

Snap off the woody ends of the asparagus and discard. Peel the spears with a vegetable peeler just up to their tips.

Boil water in a wide pan and add the asparagus. Cook for 4 minutes, then immediately remove from the water and douse in a bowl of cold water. Drain and pat dry.

Boil some water for the eggs in a medium saucepan. Reduce to a simmer and lower the eggs into the water. For a runny yolk, cook the eggs for 4 minutes. For a yolk the consistency of custard, cook for 5 minutes. Using a slotted spoon, remove the eggs and run them under cold water for 30 seconds.

To plate the dishes, place one soft-boiled egg in each egg cup and slice off the top with an egg topper or serrated knife. With a small spoon, gently swirl ¼ teaspoon lemon juice into the top of the yolk of each egg, add a tiny amount of salt and pepper, and stir again. Lay four spears of asparagus on each plate and squeeze the half lemon over them. Serve hot.

FAIENCE POTTERY

Faience is earthenware pottery with colorful glazes in the hues of Provence. It is made in many towns in the area because the region has a large natural supply of clay. The colors seen most often are emerald green, mustard, white, and the more poetic variety from the village of Moustiers with its delicate blue-and-white pastoral motifs.

My friend Pamela and I found my sunshine yellow faience plates in the village of Apt, and I serve my Asparagus with Soft-Boiled Egg Dip on them. I also found decorative jugs and serving platters nearby in Picasso's beloved village of Vallauris, where he lived and learned how to make pottery, producing thousands of items over the years. The pottery in Vallauris is flamboyant and playful, much of it resembling Picasso's original designs.

Naked Meat Balls
Les Tout Nus

Usually made very small, as if they were to be the filling for ravioli but without the dough, *tout nus* are often presented with a drizzle of olive oil and some grated cheese. They are always made with spinach, rice, and ground meat. This is what I was told by the best-looking waiter I have ever seen, so I listened very carefully!

Why were we on the topic of naked meatballs? I was ordering lunch in a small bistro after shopping in Antibes when I saw a dish go by and smelled an aroma worth following. Gazing up at the waiter, I asked what it was. He smiled and announced in French and English, *"Tout nus!* Naked meatballs!" He told me it was a traditional Niçoise dish that the owner's mother made for the restaurant on special days, and this was my lucky day. Would I like some? *Mais oui!*

What I loved about them was that they had a slight sweetness, a hint of orange, and they were topped not with olive oil and cheese but with a rich tomato sauce spiked with red wine.

I said my farewell, waived my thanks to the owner's mother peering around the kitchen door, and when I was a few steps away took out a piece of paper and a pen and wrote down my immediate impressions of what I thought the recipe might be.

I have arrived at a happy place. My naked meatballs taste pretty close to the restaurant's, helped along by the addition of a little orange marmalade. I like to make mine larger, serving four per person in a row on a rectangular plate, with some tomato sauce ladled down the side to drag them through before eating. The only thing missing is a handsome waiter.

Makes 24 medium-size meatballs

³/₄ cup water

¹/₄ cup rice

2 tablespoons extra virgin olive oil

1 small onion, minced

1¹/₂ teaspoons sugar

4 cloves garlic, minced, divided

1 (28-ounce) can crushed tomatoes

3 teaspoons fine sea salt, divided

¹/₂ pound ground beef

¹/₂ pound ground pork

1 (9-ounce) package frozen spinach, thawed, squeezed very dry

2 eggs, beaten

2 tablespoons orange marmalade

¹/₂ cup fresh breadcrumbs

¹/₂ cup all-purpose flour

In a saucepan, bring water to a boil, add ¼ cup rice, cover, and reduce to simmer. Cook rice till tender, about 20 minutes. Drain and set aside.

In another saucepan, heat olive oil; add the onion and cook about 3 minutes. Add the sugar and cook on medium-high another 5 minutes, until the onion turns light brown.

Add 1 clove minced garlic, tomatoes, and 1 teaspoon salt; simmer for 15 minutes. Keep warm until ready to serve.

Preheat oven to 375 degrees F. Lightly coat a baking dish with cooking spray or olive oil.

In a large bowl, add the cooked rice, ground beef, ground pork, spinach, eggs, marmalade, remaining garlic, 2 teaspoons salt, and breadcrumbs. Mix with clean hands until very well blended.

Place the flour on a large plate. Roll the meat into the size meatballs you would like (about 1 to 1½ tablespoons of meat), rolling them lightly without compacting too much. Then roll each meatball in the flour and shake off any excess.

Place the meatballs on the baking dish, put into the oven, and bake for 16 minutes, or until done. If you make them smaller, bake for 8 to 10 minutes.

To serve, spread a little sauce on a plate and set the meatballs in the sauce, or alternatively, line them down a plate and serve with a small bowl of sauce to dunk them in.

PISTACHIO PARMESAN CHICKPEA FRIES
Les Panisses

Recipe by recipe, I cooked my way through the cookbook written by Nice's former mayor. I later found one other source, *The Cuisine of the Sun* by Mireille Johnston, a lovely cookbook that included many recipes from Nice; but the former mayor's book was the only one I could track down that focused exclusively on the authentic style of cooking I was so keen to learn. In many ways, I felt privileged to have found a copy of his book, and to be able to also follow the trail left by recipes given to my neighbors and friends by their mothers, grandmothers and great-grandmothers.

A recipe for *panisses* from the former mayor's book became an instant favorite because it resembles french fries but uses chickpea flour, which produces a wonderful flavor. According to the mayor, the traditional way to make panisses fries is to pour the chickpea batter into a series of well-oiled saucers to cool, then slice the firm batter into french fries. I find a square cake pan or gratin dish works as well.

Makes 42 fries

4 cups water

2 1/4 cups chickpea flour

1 teaspoon extra virgin olive oil

1/4 teaspoon turmeric

2 teaspoons salt

pinch of cayenne pepper, or more

6 cracks of freshly ground black pepper

1/4 cup salted pistachios, finely ground

1/2 cup grated Parmesan or Pecorino Romano cheese

oil for frying

fine sea salt

freshly ground black pepper

Choose a 9 x 9-inch baking pan, a gratin dish, or 12 saucers. If using a square cake pan or gratin dish, line it with plastic wrap, then oil the plastic wrap on the bottom and up the sides, leaving the plastic wrap to hang over the sides. If following the saucer method, oil a dozen saucers.

In a large saucepan, place the water, chickpea flour, oil, turmeric, salt, cayenne to taste, and pepper. Whisk until well combined. Cook over medium heat for 6 to 7 minutes, stirring constantly with a whisk. Stir in the pistachios and cheese. Switch to a wooden spoon and stir vigorously for 2 minutes, first in one direction, then in the other, until the batter becomes very thick and bubbly and is pulling away from the sides of the pan.

Spoon the mixture into the saucers or baking pan and allow to cool enough that you can smooth out the top of the batter with your oiled fingers. Let sit at room temperature for 8 minutes. Remove the cooled mixture to a cutting board and, with an oiled knife, slice into slim rectangles, 1/2 inch wide and 3 inches long.

Fill a large skillet or wide saucepan with enough olive oil to reach halfway up the fries, and heat to sizzling hot, between 365 and 375 degrees F. Use tongs to carefully lower the fries into the hot oil. Cook in batches until brown on all sides, about 3 minutes. You want them brown, not burned, so they are crispy on the outside and creamy on the inside. Drain on paper towels, and shower fries with sea salt and lots of pepper. Serve hot.

Note: If you would like to leave out the pistachios and cheese, the recipe works just as well without them.

STEPHAN'S FISH TOASTS
Les Tartines aux Rougets

Leaving my car in the driveway, I entered the olive mill, with its cool stone interior and massive antique grinding stone.

After a few moments of amazement at the cavernous showroom and all the products made from olives stacked everywhere, I filled my jug with oil, claimed a couple of jars of local olives and a jar or two of tapenade, and headed home. All that was needed would be to stop at the village baker for a baguette and at the wine store for rosé.

A candle lit. A sip of wine. A plate of olives. Another perfect night was beginning.

After the wine and olives, I sat everyone down at the dining room table and brought out the appetizer—a recipe for fish toasts given to me by my friend and private chef Stephan Smith.

Fish toasts are easy and quick to make and unusual enough to draw smiles when they come to the table. Pick them up and eat them! Slathered with dark olive tapenade and topped with delightful small sautéed fish bites, they take the notion of comfort food to great heights.

Serves 4

1 pound firm-flesh fish fillets
  (e.g., red mullet or tilapia)

4 tablespoons extra virgin
  olive oil, divided

2 teaspoons Cognac

1 (8-ounce) jar olive tapenade

8 slices white or sourdough
  bread, toasted, sliced into
  rectangles, crusts removed

8 basil leaves

With scissors, cut the fish fillets into long pieces that look as if they will fit nicely on top of your toast rectangles.

Heat 3 tablespoons olive oil in a skillet until hot, then sauté the fish until just done, about 3 minutes.

Mix the Cognac into the tapenade.

Spread each toast rectangle with tapenade, top with a piece of fish, and arrange artfully on a platter.

Decorate with fresh basil leaves and serve while still warm.

MOULIN D'OPIO

The variety of olives found in the area of the Alpes-Maritimes around Nice is called "la caillette." They are small black or purple ovals when ripe and produce an oil with a subtle taste and golden color. At Moulin d'Opio, a seven-generation family-run mill, oil is made from local olives brought by small producers and individuals living nearby.

Moulin d'Opio Olive Mill
2, route de Châteauneuf
06650 Opio
Telephone: (33) 04 93 77 23 03
www.moulin-dopio.com

UNCLE JOHNS
Barba Jouan

One specialty of the French Riviera is small fried turnovers called *barba jouan* (Uncle Johns), which are offered with a glass of wine or served as a snack. In the winter they are stuffed with pumpkin, rice, and grated Parmesan; in summer, Swiss chard, leeks, rice, *brousse* (ricotta), and Parmesan. Sometimes there are bits of cooked ground meat or ham in them.

My Uncle Johns are baked in store-bought puff pastry and stuffed with a mild butternut squash filling. (*Tip:* You can often find raw butternut squash precut and packaged.)

Serve them with a small bowl of crispy, salted fried sage leaves on the side, a perfect pairing to the butternut filling.

If you would like to fry the barba jouan instead, as is traditional, make them with egg pasta dough, stuff them as you would ravioli, then gently drop into 360-degree F. vegetable oil for 3 to 4 minutes, until golden.

Makes 24

1 package puff pastry, thawed

1 cup water

¼ cup brown rice

7 tablespoons olive oil, divided

2 tablespoons sugar

½ teaspoon cinnamon

2 cups cubed raw butternut squash

½ cup whole milk ricotta cheese

1 egg, beaten

1¼ cups grated Pecorino Romano cheese

1 teaspoon salt

¼ teaspoon freshly ground black pepper

dash of cayenne pepper

2 sprigs fresh thyme, leaves minced

egg wash: 1 egg beaten
with 1 teaspoon water

20-25 fresh sage leaves

salt

Heat the oven to 400 degrees F. Lightly oil a baking sheet.

Unfold the thawed puff pastry, cover with plastic wrap, and keep cool in the refrigerator until ready to roll out.

Bring water and rice to a boil; reduce to simmer and cook for 30 minutes. Drain.

Whisk 2 tablespoons olive oil with the sugar and cinnamon and pour over the cubes of squash, using your hands to toss and coat them. Spread the squash cubes out on the baking sheet, and bake for 20 to 25 minutes. Let cool, then mash with a fork, potato masher, or in a food processor, but do not purée; leave some small pieces in the mix.

In a large bowl, place the ricotta, egg, cheese, salt, black pepper, rice, butternut squash, 1 tablespoon olive oil, cayenne pepper, and thyme. Mix well with a fork.

Unfold the pastry sheets and place one on a sheet of parchment paper. Place some plastic wrap over the other sheet to keep it from drying. Roll the pastry sheet out to 10 by 13 inches, and then cut into 3-inch circles with a wine glass or cookie cutter, to yield 12 circles.

Place 1 teaspoon of filling in the center of each circle, pull the top over to form a semicircle, and press the edges firmly to seal. Press the edges again with a fork. Place the pastries on a baking sheet lined with parchment paper.

Repeat process with the other pastry sheet. Prick each pastry once with a fork, then brush with the egg wash. Bake for 15 to 20 minutes, until golden.

For the fried sage leaves, heat 4 tablespoons olive oil in a small skillet until shimmering hot, add the sage leaves, and fry for about 30 seconds, until crisp. Any longer, and they will brown. Transfer to paper towels, sprinkle with salt, and cool. Serve in a small bowl beside the barba jouans.

MINI PAN BAGNAT
Le Pan Bagnat Amuse-Gueule

Driving along the coastal road to Nice airport to pick up our first overseas visitors, I spied a food truck parked on the beach and a Mercedes parked right next to it. I was an hour early and hungry, so I pulled in next to the Mercedes, just as a woman emerged from the car and walked towards the food truck.

This was a *pan bagnat* truck, one of many that arrive on or near the beach around lunchtime. After waiting in line a few minutes, the lady turned, carrying a stack of four huge pan bagnat wrapped like presents in paper and tied with twine. She smiled as if she were carrying a prize and said, "The best pan bagnat on the coast!"

I agreed. From then on, when I saw that particular truck, I would swerve off the road. There was something about the way the dressing was made. And each and every ingredient was startlingly fresh.

Pan bagnat is a simple sandwich from Nice, which translated means "bathed bread," and bakers in Nice produce a roll specifically for making it. Waverley Root described it in *The Food of France* as Nice's beach picnic food, eaten between dips in the Mediterranean Sea.

It's like a Salade Niçoise sandwiched between two slices of a large, bulky roll that soaks up the juices from the tomatoes and vinaigrette. This miniaturized version is an invitation to the table, a small, delectable bite before the evening meal. Wrap yours twice with twine and tie with a bow or simple knot.

Makes 8

4   medium eggs

1   cup extra virgin olive oil

6   tablespoons red or white wine vinegar

¼   teaspoon sugar

10   anchovy fillets, minced

     pinch of freshly ground black pepper

2   cloves garlic

6   ounces cherry tomatoes, sliced

6   ounces mesclun salad (or
     soft butter lettuce)

1   scallion, thinly sliced

½   green bell pepper, seeded, finely diced

6   large basil leaves, minced

8   small rolls or buns (the
     smallest you can find)

1   small jar black olive tapenade

1   (5-ounce) can solid light tuna
     in olive oil, best quality

Place the eggs in a saucepan and pour cold water over them to cover by 1 inch. Bring the water to a boil, then remove the pan from the stove, cover, and leave for 10 minutes. Move eggs to a bowl of cold water and ice cubes to cool; then peel and slice.

In a bowl, whisk together the olive oil, vinegar, sugar, anchovies, and pepper. Press or finely mince the garlic and whisk into the vinaigrette. Add the cherry tomatoes and toss with a fork. Allow to rest for 15 minutes for the juice from the tomatoes to work into the vinaigrette. Then remove the tomatoes to a medium-size bowl.

To the medium-size bowl with the tomatoes, add the salad leaves, scallion, green pepper, and basil. Pour only enough of the remaining vinaigrette over the top to toss and coat the salad. Reserve the leftover vinaigrette.

Slice the rolls in half and scoop out some of the soft interior. With a pastry brush, paint the insides of the rolls with a little of the remaining vinaigrette, then thinly spread tapenade on the bottom half.

Drain the tuna and reserve the oil. Lightly mash the tuna with a fork to soften, adding drops of oil from the can if needed.

Fill each roll with the salad mix, top with the tuna and then egg slices, and drizzle a couple of drops of olive oil and red wine vinegar on the top. Place the tops on the sandwiches and press down firmly.

To serve, tie each little roll twice around with kitchen twine, then tie a bow. Arrange on a serving platter and allow the pan bagnat to rest for an hour before serving, for the flavors to combine.

SOUPS

Les Soupes

Cantaloupe Soup with Raw Beet Salad
La Soupe de Melon avec une Salade de Betteraves Crues

The people that find their way to the open-air markets—from the burly-armed farmers who delicately arrange their strawberries and radishes in tableaus worthy of a Dutch still-life painting to the shoppers fully expecting surprise encounters as they discover a new source for fresh cheese or mountain honey—all come together for the celebration of food.

Within this sacred communion, I joined with abandon bordering on gaiety a tradition that has been part of French life since the Middle Ages. I mean, where else can you find perfectly ripe peaches like these? I could smell them a stall away. And that honey smell. What was that? Then I would spy to my left a pale green pyramid of perfectly balanced Cavaillon melons, so ripe and ready to eat they were bursting for attention. Cavaillon melons, similar to cantaloupe, always have a place in my basket when I come home from these markets. They taste indescribably sweet and delicious. That sweetness and the spirit of the open-air market star in this ethereal soup.

Serves 4

1 medium-size raw beet, peeled

4 tablespoons extra virgin olive oil, divided

1 teaspoon white vinegar

$1/2$ teaspoon salt, divided

4 cups tightly packed sliced fresh cantaloupe

1 cup water

4 teaspoons sugar

Coarsely grate the beet on a box grater into a bowl.

In another small bowl, whisk together 2 tablespoons olive oil, vinegar, and $1/4$ teaspoon salt. Pour over the grated beets and mix well. Reserve.

Place the cantaloupe in a blender with water, $1/4$ teaspoon salt, sugar, and 2 tablespoons olive oil. Blend for 3 minutes, until silky smooth.

Pour the soup into four bowls. Spoon equal portions of beet salad onto the center of each bowl of soup and serve.

ELEMENTS OF A NIÇOISE SOUP

There are certain elements, when put together, that differentiate Niçoise soups.

Fragrance is one. For hot soups, the scent of fresh herbs should drift to your nose; so herbs are left raw and snipped over soup at the very last minute to allow the heat of the soup to release their aroma and encourage their fragrance to rise. *Pistou*—a raw blend of basil, garlic, and Parmesan—when swirled into hot soup, radiates a smell that excites your taste buds before you even raise a spoonful of the soup to your lips.

Texture is another important element. Before serving many soups, a piece of toast will be added in the bottom of the bowl for a substantive layer, while a final shower of grated cheese will melt, adding silkiness.

For chilled, puréed soups, the addition of one or two tablespoonfuls of olive oil while blending emulsifies the soup and gives it a luxuriously smooth feel in the mouth. This is in contrast to the more traditional *velouté* soups, which require a roux or cream for their silkiness.

Niçoise soups are also a part of the Niçoise home cook's skills for making culinary curatives. Knowledgeable about the medicinal qualities of herbs native to the region, home cooks thoughtfully prepare healthful soups for their families. They speak of adding rosemary to the soup to destroy microorganisms, sage to help with digestion, and garlic to make the heart strong and clean the blood—bringing the natural herbal pharmacy existing around them into the home.

Because of the wealth of olives in the region, a judicious drizzle of exquisitely fragrant, best-quality extra virgin olive oil is a frequent and comforting flourish before serving a soup.

CLOUDLIKE CHICKEN BASIL LEMON SOUP
La Soupe "Comme un Nuage" de Poulet, Citron et Basilic

Free-range, farm-bred chickens rotate in rotisserie machines at shops everywhere in France. Some of the shops specialize in birds from different regions, some in local birds. Some lay sliced potatoes at the bottom of the rotisserie so they become infused with the dripping chicken fat; these are offered as a side dish. Some ask if you would like the drippings as well. *Heaven*.

I often buy a rotisserie chicken to make this quick, flavorful soup, especially when the fat, juicy Menton lemons come into season.

Serves 6

1 store-bought rotisserie chicken

8 cups chicken broth

1 tablespoon minced fresh basil leaves, plus 6 leaves for garnish

3 cloves garlic, minced

¾ cup orzo

2 lemons, zested and juiced

salt

4 eggs, room temperature, separated

Take the meat off the chicken and slice into small pieces or pull with a fork to shred. Keep 3 cups for this soup and refrigerate any remaining chicken for sandwiches.

Place the chicken broth, minced basil, and garlic in a saucepan and bring to a boil. Add the orzo and simmer until it is cooked. Add 4 tablespoons lemon juice and salt to taste. Add more lemon juice if you would like a more lemony flavor. Remove from the heat.

Beat the egg yolks until thick and pale.

In another bowl, beat the egg whites until stiff. Gently fold the egg whites into the egg yolks until blended, taking care to keep the volume.

Whisk a fourth of the egg mixture into the soup until combined. Quickly whisk in the rest of the egg mixture and return to the heat for a few seconds, still whisking, trying to preserve its volume and foam.

Divide the chicken among six bowls. Ladle the soup over the top and serve with a little bit of the lemon zest in the center. With scissors, cut 1 basil leaf per bowl over the lemon zest, and serve.

CREAMLESS CREAMY CHICKPEA AND SAGE PURÉE
La Purée de Pois Chiches à la Sauge sans Crème

There was a luminous glow from a full moon behind the clouds one winter night, and within the small stone-walled restaurant, candles flickered. A chalkboard outside announced the menu, starting with *velouté de pois chiches* (a chickpea soup). As I began to imagine what it might taste like, snow began to fall.

It's rare to see snow on the Côte d'Azur, and when it was falling in the stunningly picturesque village of Valbonne, it was an event worth capturing. As my husband pulled out his camera, I pushed open the door of the restaurant. He soon joined me, with snowflakes on his shoulders.

The soup warmed and charmed us. It was so perfectly right for that snowy night. Served steaming hot from an heirloom soup tureen, it had a creamy texture; but I was told there was no cream in it. This is my version, a winter warmer with sage.

Makes 4 cups

10 fresh sage leaves

1 large carrot, sliced

2 (15.5-ounce) cans chickpeas, drained

1 (14.5-ounce) can chicken or vegetable broth

4 tablespoons fresh lemon juice

1 clove garlic, sliced

1 1/2 teaspoons salt

1/4 teaspoon black pepper

1 tablespoon extra virgin olive oil

optional: 8 sage leaves for garnish

Roll the 10 sage leaves tightly, cut into slices, and add to a blender or food processor. Add the carrot, chickpeas, broth, lemon juice, garlic, salt, pepper, and olive oil. Purée until smooth.

Pour the purée into a saucepan and cook on medium-low heat until the soup comes to a simmer. Ladle into shallow soup bowls and serve.

Note: To garnish, fry fresh sage leaves in very hot olive oil for just a few seconds to crisp them. Remove them with a slotted spoon to a paper towel, sprinkle with salt, and place in the center of each bowl.

Tip: For a fancier garnish, smear 4 sage leaves with anchovy paste, press the other 4 sage leaves on top, and fry until crisp but not brown.

Madame's Spinach, Pea, and Pecorino Romano Soup
La Soupe de Madame aux Épinards, aux Petits Pois, et au Pecorino Romano

The grinding of gears in my neighbor's ancient Citroën announced her arrival. I threw open the front door to see her walking towards me with a large pot.

"I heard you were not feeling well, so I brought you some soup. The same soup my mother used to make for me when I was a child."

And then, with waving arms and hands, she was gone. No doubt a smart move, after seeing how I looked. And no doubt, this soup made me feel better.

Serves 4

6 ounces fresh baby spinach

4 cups water

1 1/2 teaspoons salt

1/4 teaspoon coarsely ground black pepper, plus more for serving

1 clove garlic

2 cups frozen peas

2 egg yolks, beaten

8 tablespoons ground Pecorino Romano cheese, plus 1/2 cup for serving

In a food processor, add the spinach, water, salt, pepper, and garlic. Process for 60 seconds.

Pour into a saucepan; add the peas and bring to a boil. Turn down to a simmer and cook for 3 minutes. Take the soup off the heat and quickly whisk in the egg yolks and cheese for about 1 minute, until well blended.

Ladle soup into bowls. Pass extra cheese and place a pepper mill nearby.

SHRIMP AND FISH SOUP WITH TOAST AND ROUILLE
La Purée de Crevettes et Poisson avec du Pain Grillé et de la Rouille

Through the window beside our table we could see a female sun worshiper studiously applying suntan lotion to her ample topless chest. I heard a little scream escape from my mother-in-law, who was sitting demurely across the table from me. We were at Nounou, a traditional fish restaurant located on the beach. It was to be a special treat, a leisurely, formal Sunday lunch before we took her sightseeing on a gloriously sunny day. I guess I had forgotten to tell her that topless bathing is acceptable in the South of France.

Looking across at her distraught face, I noticed just a glimmer of humor begin to appear in her eyes, and then she laughed and held the menu up to hide her face. Whew! Crisis averted. I began to chat away about the etiquette involved in eating the soup we had ordered for the table—hoping to distract her from looking out the window.

We had brought her to what had become one of our favorite beach restaurants to try one of the most popular soups along the Côte d'Azur, *soupe de poisson.* When you order it, plates are set before you with toasted slices of baguette, bowls of *rouille* sauce, grated cheese, and a plate with raw halves of garlic. I explained that there is a sequence of events involved in eating this soup. First, she should take a piece of toasted baguette, rub it with the raw garlic, smear it with some of the rouille, and then place the bread in the bottom of her bowl—which we all did. The soup arrived and was ladled over our toasts. I then had her follow my lead and shower the top of her soup with the grated Emmental cheese. She loved it. She even took another peek at the lady on the beach and looked back at me with a mischievous smile, "What a beautiful view!"

To make a true soupe de poisson, like that found at Nounou, requires local fish not easily found elsewhere. It also requires fish heads, tails, eel, and other bits and bobs that complicate matters. To simplify, I came up with a recipe that approximates soupe de poisson. Ideally, you would make it with 4 cups of fish stock, but unless you have access to a good fish market that can provide you with the fixings to make it, you can substitute shrimp stock. Cook the shrimp, keep the broth, peel them, and add the shrimp to the blender when you process the soup; this gives you a thick shrimp-flavored soup that is a meal in itself. Sunbather optional.

Serves 4

continued >

FOR THE ROUILLE

5 large cloves garlic

1 roasted red pepper from a jar

1 small fresh red chili pepper, seeded and sliced

1 egg yolk

1 teaspoon salt

1 slice white bread, crusts removed, torn into pieces

1 1/2 tablespoons fresh lemon juice

1/2 cup extra virgin olive oil

FOR THE SOUP

1 pound medium shrimp, unpeeled

4 cups water

2 tablespoons extra virgin olive oil

2 pounds white fish fillets

1 cup dry white wine

2 carrots, thinly sliced

2 stalks celery, thinly sliced

1 onion, thinly sliced

4 tomatoes, peeled, seeded and chopped

2 tablespoons tomato paste

1 tablespoon Cognac or Pernod

4 cloves garlic, peeled and sliced

2 sprigs fresh thyme, leaves only

1 teaspoon salt

dash of cayenne pepper

16 slices baguette, divided

2 large cloves garlic, peeled and halved

1 cup freshly grated Emmental cheese

First, make the rouille by turning on a food processor and dropping in the garlic cloves to mince them. Turn off and add the roasted red pepper, chili pepper, egg yolk, salt, bread and lemon juice; process for 60 seconds. With the machine running, drip in the olive oil very slowly to make a mayonnaise consistency. Set aside or refrigerate the rouille until ready to use.

Next, in a large saucepan, cook shrimp in the water until they are pink and the water has taken on the flavor of the shrimp. Remove shrimp, reserving the water in the saucepan. Peel the shrimp and place them in a blender or food processor. (Reserve 4 to 8 shrimp for garnish if you wish.)

Heat olive oil in a skillet and fry the fish until lightly browned.

To the shrimp water, add the fish, wine, carrots, celery, onion, tomatoes, tomato paste, Cognac or Pernod, sliced garlic, thyme, salt, and cayenne. Bring to a boil, then turn the heat down, cover, and simmer for 20 minutes.

Add everything to the blender or food processor that holds the shrimp, a cup at a time, to purée. (Be careful when adding hot liquid to a blender, as it expands and can splatter. Try holding a kitchen towel over the lid when you turn it on.) If your blender does not hold the entire amount, work in batches, pouring each batch of puréed soup back into the saucepan. Add a bit more water if it is too thick, and bring to a simmer. Taste for seasoning and add salt if you wish.

Lightly toast slices of baguette. Rub four of them with the cut side of the halved garlic and place in the bottom of individual soup bowls. Spread a spoonful of rouille on top of each toast, ladle the hot soup over, and shower with freshly grated cheese. Offer extra baguette slices, rouille, and grated cheese on the side. If you offer extra garlic, slice in half, leaving the skin on to protect fingers from garlic. A nice garnish would be to add a couple of shrimp in the center of each bowl.

Restaurant Nounou
Boulevard des Frères Roustan
06220 Golfe-Juan
Telephone: (33) 04 93 63 71 73
www.nounou.fr

CELERY ROOT RÉMOULADE SOUP WITH CELERY LEAF SALAD
La Soupe de "Céleri-rave Rémoulade" avec sa Salade de Feuilles de Céleri

From the time we lived in Paris when I was a newlywed, I have had a love affair with the salad called *céleri-rave rémoulade*.

I woke up at our house one morning thinking about it, with the next thought being what to make for lunch, and somehow the idea of making a light and creamy soup that tasted like my favorite salad seemed like an interesting idea to play with. Now I have two ways of enjoying it!

Serves 4

1 large celery root (celeriac)

2³/4 teaspoons fine sea salt, divided

1/2 cup onion, finely chopped

2 tablespoons lemon juice

2 teaspoons Dijon mustard

2 egg yolks

1/4 cup extra virgin olive oil, plus 3 tablespoons for the celery leaf salad

1 tablespoon white or sherry vinegar

leaves from 1 bunch celery

Slice the celery root in half, and with the flat side down, peel off the outer skin with a small knife. Slice the celery root thinly, slice again in halves, and then chop (you should have about 3 to 4 cups). Add to a large saucepan, cover with water, and add 1 teaspoon salt. Cover and bring to a boil; then turn down and simmer for 35 minutes, until very tender.

Transfer the celery root to a blender with 2 cups of the cooking water, and purée. Pour into a large bowl.

To the bowl of a food processor, add the onion, lemon juice, mustard, 1 1/2 teaspoons salt, and 1/2 cup of the purée; process until smooth.

In another bowl, beat the egg yolks until thick and light. Slowly drizzle in 1/8 cup olive oil, drop by drop as you beat, until it starts to thicken; then slowly drizzle in the rest of the oil until it reaches mayonnaise consistency. Add the onion-lemon juice mixture to the egg mixture, and beat to blend.

Scoop the egg mixture into the celery root purée and whisk to combine. Taste for seasoning, adding more salt if needed.

Whisk 3 tablespoons olive oil, vinegar, and 1/4 teaspoon salt together. Choose only the palest green and smallest celery leaves if you can. Drizzle just enough of the vinaigrette over them to coat. Toss well.

Ladle the soup into four bowls, then top with a mound of celery leaf salad in the middle. Serve hot or cold.

ABOUT CELERY ROOT

This ugliest of ugly vegetables, *celeriac*, tastes more intensely like celery than celery does and is worth getting to know better. It's loaded with fiber, Vitamin K, and has only 30 calories per half cup. Look for firm bulbs without discoloration. To use it, wash, clean, and peel. Try it raw in salads or puréed as an alternative to mashed potatoes.

Sébastien Broda's Cream of Pumpkin Soup with Lemon
La Velouté de Potiron au Citron de Sébastien Broda

Host to the Cannes Film Festival, Cannes is a city by the sea, where movie stars are seen shopping in stores along the Croisette and sipping espresso late at night at its outdoor cafés. Their hand prints are embedded in the sidewalk outside the Festival Hall and their glamour seems to linger on until the festival the next year.

In addition to the stars, a chef has achieved billboard status as well. Sébastien Broda, chef at Le Park45 Restaurant, has become the face of Cannes from a culinary point of view. His approach is still that of the traditional Niçoise philosophy and style of cooking, but he is one of the young chefs taking it to its next evolutionary leap. This is Sébastien's recipe for a light pumpkin soup with intriguing undertones of candied lemon.

Serves 4

4 large organic lemons

9 cups water, divided

7 tablespoons sugar, divided

1 fresh small Sugar Baby pumpkin
   or butternut squash

2 white onions, thinly sliced

1 1/2 cups milk

2 tablespoons olive oil

3/4 teaspoon salt

   freshly ground pepper

Le Park45 Restaurant
At Le Grand Hotel
45 Bd. de La Croisette
06414 Cannes
Telephone: (33) 04 93 38 15 45
www.grand-hotel-cannes.com

Wash and dry the lemons. With a vegetable peeler, peel them.

Bring 3 cups water to a simmer, drop in the lemon peels, and simmer for 2 minutes. Drain into a colander, discarding the water. Add 3 cups fresh water to the pot, bring to a simmer, drop in the lemon peels, and simmer for 2 minutes. Do this one more time, so that you have blanched and drained the peels three times.

Squeeze the juice from 4 lemons and place it in a saucepan with 7 tablespoons sugar. Over medium heat, whisk until the sugar is dissolved; then add the lemon peels, turn down the heat to low, and cook until an instant-read thermometer registers 230 to 235 degrees F. Remove from the heat and set aside.

To prepare the pumpkin, slice it into long, thin wedges, as you would a melon. Scrape out the stringy insides and seeds. Peel away and discard the rind. (I place a wedge of pumpkin on a kitchen towel skin side down to anchor it, then use a small serrated knife in a sawing motion from one end of the wedge to the other to remove the rind.) Dice the flesh until you have 5 cups of tightly packed pumpkin. Save any leftover for another meal, or freeze it in a plastic bag.

Add pumpkin to a large soup pot with the onions and cover with water. Bring to a boil, then turn down the heat to medium-low; cover and cook slowly for 1/2 hour, until tender. Drain the water from the pumpkin and onions, place them in a food processor or blender, in two batches if needed, and purée.

Add the lemon peels with syrup, milk, and olive oil; purée until smooth. Add 3/4 teaspoon salt and pepper to taste; then pour back into the soup pot. Heat the soup, ladle into bowls, and serve.

Chilled Red Pepper, Orange, and Yogurt Soup with Parsley Salad

La Soupe Glacée de Poivron Rouge et Yaourt à l'Orange avec sa Salade de Persil

My friend Anna was visiting from the States, and I knew that she had been on a raw diet for months. Rather than have her completely veer off track, I created some raw dishes for her during the week she stayed with me.

She arrived during a torridly hot time, when all we could think about was keeping the wooden shutters closed to keep out the heat and eating everything chilled. I came up with this hydrating, refreshing soup that I put in a thermos and took with me to the airport. I wanted her first visit to France to be magical, so I picked her up and drove her to a stretch of beach facing the pale azure sea, spread out a blanket, poured the cold soup into two mugs, and we had soup with a view.

I serve it at home with a mound of parsley salad in the center.

Serves 4

2 large red bell peppers, seeded and sliced

2 organic oranges

1 cup water

3/4 teaspoon fine sea salt, divided

3 teaspoons sugar

1/2 cup Greek yogurt

1 1/2 cups flat leaf parsley, leaves only

3 teaspoons olive oil

1 1/2 teaspoons red wine vinegar

Place the peppers in the bowl of a food processor or blender.

Grate the rind of 1 orange and reserve. Peel the second orange. Slice the white pith off both oranges, then slice the oranges and add to the food processor or blender. Add 1 cup water, 1/4 teaspoon salt, and sugar. Process for at least 60 seconds.

Add the yogurt and process, then pour into a large soup bowl or individual serving bowls.

In a mixing bowl, toss the parsley leaves, 3 tablespoons of the grated orange rind, oil, vinegar, and 1/2 teaspoon salt with a fork until well blended. Taste and add more salt if needed.

Spoon the salad onto the center of each bowl of soup before serving.

VEGETABLE PISTOU SOUP
La Soupe au Pistou

The wife of the retired chief of police in our village gave me a recipe for *lou pistou.* I learned her basic recipe, then used whatever vegetables were at hand in my garden or the market to make it. Once you prep all the vegetables, you are good to go and the recipe moves quite quickly.

The soup is named after the pistou sauce you spoon onto the soup in each bowl. The pistou does not cook but rather warms and releases its basil and garlic aroma. A generous grating of Emmental cheese and passed basket of warm, sliced baguette finishes the meal. Why Emmental? The region around Nice, at the base of the Alpes-Maritimes, favors using Swiss Emmental cheese, which melts into the hot soup.

Serves 4-6

FOR THE SOUP

6 cups chicken or vegetable stock (traditionally, water)

3 tablespoons extra virgin olive oil, plus more for drizzling

1 medium potato, unpeeled, diced

1 medium onion, coarsely chopped

2 medium carrots, 1 diced, 1 grated

5 cloves garlic, minced

2 tablespoons rice

1 (15-ounce) can cannellini beans, drained

½ pound string beans, ends removed, sliced in 8 pieces

2 cups Swiss chard leaves, coarsely chopped

1½ teaspoons fine sea salt

freshly ground pepper

4 Roma tomatoes, seeded, diced

3 teaspoons fresh thyme, chopped

2 basil leaves, finely chopped

2 cups freshly grated Emmental cheese

warmed baguette

FOR THE PISTOU

3 large cloves garlic, sliced in thirds

⅛ teaspoon fine sea salt

2 cups tightly packed fresh basil leaves

¼ cup extra virgin olive oil

2 tablespoons freshly grated Parmesan cheese

Bring the stock or water to a boil.

In another large pot, place 3 tablespoons olive oil, potato, onion, diced carrot, and garlic. Cook over medium heat, half covered with a lid, for 8 minutes, stirring frequently.

Pour the hot stock into the vegetables, add the rice, cannellini beans, and string beans. Bring to a boil, reduce heat, and allow to simmer gently for 20 minutes.

Meanwhile, make the pistou. Add the garlic, salt, basil, oil, and Parmesan cheese to a food processor, and pulse until well blended. Reserve.

To the soup pot, add the Swiss chard, grated carrot, salt, and pepper; simmer for 3 minutes. Taste and adjust seasonings.

Stir the tomatoes, thyme, and basil into the hot soup, and ladle the soup into bowls. Add a dollop of pistou in the center, a drizzle of extra virgin olive oil around the outer edges, and the grated Emmental cheese all over the top. Serve with hunks or slices of warmed baguette.

ABOUT LA SOUPE AU PISTOU

Traditional Niçoise-style pistou soup includes carrots, string beans, onions, turnips, tomatoes, zucchini, potatoes, Swiss chard, garlic, fresh green peas or broad beans or fresh white beans or fresh cranberry beans, and rice or vermicelli. It always has tomatoes, zucchini, and string beans as its anchor.

I remember Madame would sit at her kitchen table with all her vegetables spread out before her and clean and chop every one into separate bowls, aiming for variety and loads of freshly chopped herbs. Rather than measuring, she would eyeball how much liquid her vegetables demanded, sometimes arriving at quite a large pot of soup, which she would then share with extended family and neighbors. If you follow her lead and have some left over, this soup freezes beautifully. She also pounded her pistou in a mortar and pestle. Hers came out much more flavorful and fragrant than one made in a food processor.

Lentil Swiss Chard Soup with Orange Zest
La Soupe de Lentilles et Blettes au Zeste d'Orange

We love this soup at the end of the summer, when the fragrance of damp autumn leaves is in the air and there is a morning chill but still a summer sun. We serve it with our local Bellet wine and a hunk of crusty bread.

Serves 4

1¼ cups lentils du Puy

1 stalk Swiss chard, washed and patted dry

3 tablespoons extra virgin olive oil

1 small onion, diced

4 cloves garlic, finely chopped

6 cups chicken or vegetable stock

1 sprig fresh thyme, leaves only

2 strips orange rind, finely minced, plus zest of ½ orange

1 teaspoon salt

freshly ground black pepper

1 medium carrot, grated

1 small hunk Parmesan cheese

Place the lentils in a fine sieve and rinse under running water.

Slice the leaves from the Swiss chard then slice the stalk into ¼-inch pieces. Roll the leaves tightly, slice them, then finely chop.

In a soup pot, heat the olive oil and sauté the onion and garlic until translucent. Add the lentils, stock, thyme, minced orange rind, Swiss chard stalk (reserve the leaves), salt, and pepper to taste. Bring to a boil, then reduce to a simmer and cook for 30 minutes.

Add the Swiss chard leaves and grated carrot, and simmer for another 5 minutes. Add water if the soup is getting too thick. Taste and adjust salt.

Ladle into a soup tureen or individual bowls, and sprinkle with the orange zest. Serve Parmesan cheese on a small plate with a grater on the side.

ABOUT SWISS CHARD

There is no doubt that Swiss chard reigns supreme in Niçoise cooking. Its glossy, dark green leaves and multi-colored stalks, ranging from red to white to green, are used in every manner, from savory to sweet. It is enjoyed in soups, gratins, gnocchi, omelets, salads, and tarts.

RUSTIC GARLIC AND SAGE SOUP
La Soupe Campagnarde de l'Ail à la Sauge

You won't find this soup easily in a restaurant in Nice, yet it is common in the traditional Niçoise home. In the same way we think of chicken soup as a soothing remedy, garlic and sage soup is thought of as a health-giving soup, a curative for colds and hangovers.

Niçoise cuisine uses herbs for their medicinal qualities as much as for flavoring. Sage is used extensively for its digestive properties, while garlic is believed to clean the blood. This soup has an ample amount of both.

Serves 4

1   cup boiling water

12   fresh sage leaves, divided

$^1/_2$ cup extra virgin olive oil

1$^1/_2$ teaspoons salt, divided

8   cups cold water

10   whole cloves garlic, peeled, plus 2 cloves garlic, sliced

$^1/_4$ cup flat leaf parsley, minced

$^1/_4$ pound angel hair pasta

1   teaspoon salt, plus more, divided

freshly ground black pepper

1   cup freshly grated Parmesan cheese

8   slices lightly toasted baguette

In a heatproof bowl, pour the boiling water over 6 sage leaves and let sit for 1 minute. Drain, squeeze leaves dry in a paper towel, and add the sage to a blender with the olive oil. Blend for 1 minute. Pour into a saucepan over medium heat, add $^1/_2$ teaspoon salt, and cook 2 minutes. Do not allow to boil. Reserve the sage oil until ready to use.

Bring 8 cups water to a boil, and add all of the garlic. Cook on medium heat for 15 minutes.

Mince the remaining 6 sage leaves and add to the garlic soup. Add the parsley and 1 teaspoon of salt, and cook for 5 minutes. Remove the 10 cooked whole cloves of garlic and mash with a fork in a small serving bowl until smooth. Reserve.

Break the pasta into small pieces, add to the broth, and cook on medium heat for 4 to 5 minutes, or until done. Taste and adjust seasoning, adding salt and freshly ground black pepper to taste.

Ladle the soup into four bowls, drizzle drops of the sage oil on top, and serve the mashed garlic and grated cheese on the side with slices of baguette. People can add the garlic and cheese to the soup, or spread the soft garlic on a slice of baguette and sprinkle cheese on the soup.

OPEN-AIR MARKETS

Most markets are only open until just past noon, so arriving by 8:30 affords the best selection. Bring a tote or wicker basket and cash. Open-air markets in the South of France, where fruit and vegetables grow under reliably sunny skies, offer some of the best produce in the country. If you see a sign for *marché paysan*, it means a farmers market of fruit, vegetables, cheeses, bread, and flowers, while *marché provençal* means you will also find stalls selling soaps, pottery, clothing, souvenirs, and linens. Don't forget to visit the stores ringing some of the bigger markets, because they offer local products and specialties of the region, including wines, oils, jams, and pastries.

Antibes—Every morning except Monday, Cours Massena in old Antibes.

Biot—Tuesday morning, Place de General de Gaulle.

Cagnes-sur-Mer—Every morning except Monday, center of town.

Cannes—Every morning except Monday, Place Forville.

Grasse—Every morning except Sunday, Monday, and Wednesday; Place aux Aires.

Menton—Every morning at the covered market les Halles.

Nice—Every morning except Monday, Cours Saleya. Fish market every morning except Monday, Place St. François in old town.

St. Paul de Vence—Every Wednesday morning, Place du Jeu de Boules.

Tourettes-sur-Loup—Wednesday morning, Place de la Libération.

Valbonne—Friday morning, Place des Arcades.

Vallauris—Every morning except Monday, Place de l'Homme au Mouton.

Vence—Every morning except Monday, Place du Grand Jardin.

Villeneuve-Loubet—Wednesday and Saturday mornings in the village.

Monaco—International food market all day Monday to Saturday, behind Place d'Armes, Marché de la Condamine, near railroad station. Fruit, vegetables, flowers every morning at the Marché de la Condamine on Place d'Armes.

VEGETABLE SOUP OVER TOAST WITH POACHED EGG
La Soupe de Légumes sur Pain Grillé avec Oeufs Pochés

Down a dirt road, around a corner, then a quick stop in front of one of the most hallowed places in my food-loving heart. A restored old stone farmhouse is home to a lovely older British couple and their lambs, goats, and hens. He makes cheese. She sells eggs. He calls her Lady Sarah.

She named her chickens after flowers, and would call for them when I arrived. *"Marigold! Rose! Petunia! Come say hello!"*

I love the girls and their crocus-yolked just-laid eggs that crown this vegetable soup, which I make while thinking of them.

Serves 4

1 large leek

2 tablespoons extra virgin olive oil

3 cloves garlic, minced

1 Yukon gold potato

2 carrots

2 tablespoons finely chopped flat leaf parsley

3 teaspoons sea salt, plus more

8 fresh basil leaves, finely chopped

2 tomatoes, finely chopped

freshly ground black pepper, optional

1 teaspoon salt

1 teaspoon white vinegar

4 large eggs

4 thick slices baguette

Remove the tough green parts from the leek, slice the leek vertically, and clean under running water. Dry. Slice very thinly.

Heat olive oil in a soup pot and sauté leeks and garlic until tender.

Slice the potato into ¼-inch slices, then stack them. Slice into ¼-inch slices again, then turn and slice to make a small dice. Add to the pot.

Slice each carrot in half vertically, then in half again vertically. Slice crosswise into ¼-inch or smaller slices. Add to the pot.

Add the parsley and 3 teaspoons salt. Pour in just enough water to cover, and bring to a boil. Simmer until vegetables are tender, about 7 minutes.

Add the basil and tomatoes, and keep the soup warm. Taste for seasoning, adding salt and freshly ground black pepper if desired.

In a skillet, pour enough water to cover the poached eggs. Add 1 teaspoon salt and vinegar, and heat until barely simmering. Crack in the eggs, one by one, and poach for about 3 minutes, or until the whites are opaque and the eggs are set to the degree you would like them cooked. Remove eggs with a slotted spoon to a plate. Pat excess water from the plate of eggs with a paper towel.

Toast baguette slices and place one in the center of each soup bowl. Top the bread with a poached egg. Then ladle the soup around and serve. Add freshly cracked black pepper and more salt if you wish.

salads

Les Salades

ELEMENTS OF A NIÇOISE GREEN SALAD

When it comes to making a salad with greens, there are elements and traditions a Niçoise cook abides by.

They always use fresh herbs, never dried. They use the best fresh young greens and the best-quality extra virgin olive oil. If cheese is added, they use Parmesan, Pecorino Romano, or Gorgonzola.

Like Italians a few miles away across the border, the Niçoise evenly coat their salad leaves first with olive oil, then drizzle on a little lemon juice or vinegar, add salt, and toss, toss, toss, to evenly blend the flavors. A pepper mill may be placed on the table, but black pepper will not be in the salad. Oil, lemon juice or a little vinegar, and salt are the primary flavors added to the baby greens.

MESCLUN SALAD
La Salade de Mesclun

"Et voila! Mesclun de Nice!" He beamed as he handed me a brown paper bag, a trophy from a totally unexpected encounter—something I would grow to expect when I shopped in Nice at the outdoor market Cours Saleya. It was here that I learned the secret. I was informed in reverent tones by an elder tending a mound of salad that his pile of greens was called *mesclun*, and that it was invented in Nice. As I watched him gently gather the greens and place them in a paper sack, he charmed me with his earnest wish that I know this fact. Like many of his generation who grew up in this sun-kissed place, he gave due respect to the land and its harvest, intent that I, too, realize the treasure I was taking home with me.

Mesclun, he said, was originally the idea of the farmers around Nice, who would bring down from the hills their own special blends of tender greens for sale in the markets. The word *mesclun* is from the Latin word for miscellaneous. Every farmer would grow and put together the blends that they most highly prized, so everyone's mix was different. He said that one of the most authentic mixes typical of Nice, *lou mesclun*, is one that includes baby dandelion leaves, tiny leaves of young lettuce, and arugula.

The leaves should be picked that morning. And they should be just barely dressed when serving. This is my miscellaneous mix.

Serves 4

8 ounces arugula or baby spinach

1 small head of Bibb or Boston lettuce

4 radishes

¼ pound fresh raw peas

3 tablespoons extra virgin olive oil

1 tablespoon fresh lemon juice

1 tablespoon grated lemon rind

1 teaspoon fine sea salt

1 tablespoon white, wine or sherry vinegar

shavings of Parmesan cheese

Wash and dry all the greens, radishes, and peas. Slice the radishes paper thin using a mandolin or knife. Shell the peas. Place all the vegetables in a salad bowl.

Pour the olive oil over the top and toss to coat.

Whisk together the lemon juice, lemon rind, salt, and vinegar. When you are ready to serve the salad, drizzle a little on top of the greens and toss—not too much; just enough to add a veil of flavor.

At the last moment, shave some Parmesan slices with a vegetable peeler, shower them over the salad, and serve.

Candied Olive Polenta with Tomato Salad
La Polenta aux Olives Confites et sa Salade de Tomates

Once I learned how to cook with chickpea flour and to form it into *panisses*, my next quest was to become familiar with polenta the way it was cooked in Nice. I was more familiar with the wet, soft kind, but once I learned how to make polenta into solid forms that could be shaped, my imagination went wild. I put everything in it and everything on top of it. In the process, this recipe developed and stayed with me.

Prepare the polenta and allow it to cool in the refrigerator an hour ahead of composing the salad. The polenta is sublime with the addition of the candied olives, but if you prefer to save time, you can always add chopped oil-cured black olives or green olives to the mixture instead.

Serves 4

FOR THE CANDIED OLIVES

1 1/2 cups pitted canned black olives, drained

1/2 jar oil-cured black olives

1/2 cup sugar

olive oil to thin

FOR THE POLENTA

4 1/4 cups water

2 cups instant polenta

2 tablespoons extra virgin olive oil

3 teaspoons salt

freshly ground black pepper

8 tablespoons candied olives (recipe left)

FOR THE VINAIGRETTE AND SALAD

2 pounds ripe tomatoes

salt

6 tablespoons extra virgin olive oil

1 tablespoon white wine, sherry or white vinegar

1 tablespoon balsamic vinegar

1 clove garlic, pressed

1 teaspoon Dijon mustard

sea salt

1 bunch arugula, bitter salad greens, or mesclun

Line a 9 x 9-inch baking pan or gratin dish with plastic wrap that has been coated with olive oil. Leave some hanging over the side to use as handles when you transfer the polenta from the dish to a plate.

To prepare the candied olives, coarsely hand-chop the pitted canned black olives and add to a saucepan.

Squeeze the pits out of the oil-cured olives with your hands to yield about $1/2$ cup olive pieces. Add to the saucepan along with the sugar, and cook on medium to high heat to bring the mixture to a boil. Let it cook for 4 to 6 minutes. Stir in a few drops of olive oil if you would like a thinner consistency.

To prepare the polenta, boil the water in a saucepan and shower in the instant polenta, whisking constantly to prevent clumps. Stir with a wooden spoon for about 5 minutes on medium heat, until it pulls away from the sides of the pan.

Off the heat, stir in the olive oil, salt, pepper to taste, and candied olive mixture.

Spoon batter into the prepared baking pan and cool to room temperature, about 15 minutes, before covering with plastic wrap and placing in the refrigerator for 1 hour.

When you are ready to serve the salad, slice the tomatoes, place them in a colander, sprinkle with salt, toss, and let rest for 10 minutes. Rinse the salt from the tomatoes and pat dry.

Meanwhile, whisk together the olive oil, vinegars, garlic, mustard, and salt to taste, then toss the tomatoes in the dressing to coat, reserving the remaining vinaigrette in the bowl.

Slice squares of the polenta and place them on individual plates. Layer the tomatoes on top of the polenta. Toss the bitter greens in the bowl with the vinaigrette to just barely dress them, then pile them high on top of the tomatoes and serve.

ABOUT SALADE NIÇOISE

Traditionally made Salade Niçoise uses only raw vegetables, never cooked potatoes or string beans, no vinegar, and certainly not seared fresh tuna.

According to many sources, the original Salade Niçoise was made simply from tomatoes, anchovies, and olive oil. Over a hundred years, it morphed into the salad the former mayor of Nice, Jacques Médecin, codified in his cookbook. His original recipe includes the following ingredients: tomatoes, hard-boiled eggs, anchovy fillets, cucumber, green peppers, spring onions, broad beans or small artichokes, garlic, black olives, olive oil, basil leaves, and salt.

Yet, *sacré bleu!* Escoffier, who grew up on the Côte d'Azur and was a Niçoise, added string beans to his! And Julia Child, who had a house in Opio, put potato salad in hers. Neither is allowed in "real" Salade Niçoise.

TRADITIONAL SALADE NIÇOISE
La Vraie Salade Niçoise

In the eyes of the Cercle de la Capelina d'Or—the rear guard of culinary experts living around Nice and teaching cooking there—there are rules to be followed in making traditional Salade Niçoise to protect the heritage of true "cuisine Nissarde."

In honor of those who preserve traditional "cuisine Nissarde," I present you with a recipe for traditional Salade Niçoise (*la salada nissarda*), one of the most famous and loved salads in the world. Use a wooden bowl, if you can. If Niçoise olives and mesclun greens are hard to find, substitute a soft lettuce and small jarred olives.

Serves 6

8 medium-size ripe tomatoes, quartered

fine sea salt

4 green bell peppers

4 hard-boiled eggs

1 medium cucumber, peeled and sliced

2 cans light tuna in olive oil, best quality

6 tablespoons extra virgin olive oil

10 anchovy fillets, (soaked for 10 minutes and patted dry)

1 clove garlic, peeled and halved

4 cups mesclun greens

8 fresh basil leaves, chopped

3 scallions, sliced

1/4 teaspoon sea salt

4 tablespoons Niçoise olives (or best-quality jarred olives)

In a colander, generously salt the tomatoes and allow to rest while you prepare the other ingredients.

Slice the green peppers in half horizontally, then slice thinly.

Quarter the hard-boiled eggs.

Drain the oil from the canned tuna fish into a bowl with 6 tablespoons olive oil; whisk. Place the tuna on a plate and separate with a fork.

Slice the anchovy fillets into thirds.

Rub the two halves of garlic over the inside of a large wooden bowl. Lay the salad greens and basil leaves on the bottom of the bowl; top with peppers, anchovies, and scallions. Drizzle with the olive oil and sprinkle with salt. Toss to mix well.

To serve, arrange the tomatoes, eggs, cucumber, tuna, and Niçoise olives on top of the salad.

STEPHAN'S CELERY ROOT SALAD WITH RED CAVIAR
La Salade de Stephan au Céleri-rave et au Caviar Rouge

It's so easy to just buy *salade céleri rémoulade* in a tub at the supermarket in France and bring it home. But it doesn't taste anything like a freshly made celery root salad, which is crunchy and creamy all at once.

Here I present it as my friend Stephan Smith makes it: fresh, with red lumpfish. A root from the garden paired with eggs from the sea.

Serves 4

1   medium celery root (celeriac), about 1 pound

1   tablespoon lemon juice

3   teaspoons Dijon mustard

2   egg yolks

1/2   cup extra virgin olive oil

1/2   tablespoon tarragon, white, or sherry vinegar

1/4   teaspoon fine sea salt

1   tablespoon finely chopped capers

1   small jar red lumpfish or salmon eggs

2   tablespoons finely minced chives

Peel the celery root and then cut into very thin matchsticks. (If you have a shredding blade on your food processor, you can slice the celery root this way.) Transfer the celery root to a bowl and toss with lemon juice. Cover with plastic wrap and refrigerate while you make the sauce.

In a bowl and using an electric beater, beat the mustard and egg yolks until thick and pale. Slowly add half the oil, drop by drop, while beating; then add the remaining oil in a thin, steady stream while beating until you achieve mayonnaise consistency. Whisk in the vinegar and salt. Fold in the capers.

Toss the celery root matchsticks with the mayonnaise sauce, pack tightly into a small round bowl or ring mold, and invert upside down onto a plate.

Sprinkle red lumpfish or salmon eggs evenly over the top, then sprinkle with chives.

OF SALADS AND BREAD

Every morning I'd take the dogs for a long walk up the steep hill to the village for our morning baguette.

The village baker made hearty loafs—sometimes a bit on the charred side, sometimes a bit too long to be pretty, but always some of the best-tasting bread in the area. The wood burning oven was ancient, burnishing each loaf with the mystique and genes of breads made within it for over a hundred years. The burned bits were evidence that the bread was not made in a perfect modern electric oven facility, but rather shaped by hand and placed with faith inside a small inferno.

It smelled smoky and tasted so good that my dogs and I would sneak warm pieces into our mouths on the way back down the hill. It went particularly well with salads gathered from our garden later in the day.

Pamela's Pasta Salad with Chicken, Artichokes and Black Olive Pistou

La Salade de Pamela aux Pâtes, au Poulet et aux Artichauts avec le Pistou d'Olives Noires

Pamela, my English friend and a superb cook, asked me to lunch. Her husband had died years ago and she was alone, so I visited often and we planned outings around the countryside together.

Theirs must have been an amazing love affair. He was a doctor. She was a nurse. They married and moved to the South of France, where he worked from home and she helped as needed. One day she showed me a small red stone embedded into the stonework by her front door. She said, "He came back from a trip with an unpolished ruby and had it set in stone by our front door as a symbol of our love."

Pamela showed me how to cook local foods in the early days, where to source fresh goat cheese and honey between her village and mine, and where to find the best oysters in Nice. Above all, she graciously shared her recipes. This is one of them.

Serves 4

FOR THE BLACK OLIVE PISTOU

1/2 cup extra virgin olive oil

1/2 cup tightly packed basil leaves, plus 8 for garnish

3 cloves garlic, sliced

1/4 cup pitted oil-cured black olives

2 tablespoons lemon juice

1/2 cup grated Parmesan cheese

FOR THE PASTA SALAD

10 ounces pasta (e.g., penne, rigatoni, shells, or corkscrews)

1 store-bought rotisserie chicken, meat pulled off in small pieces

1 jar marinated artichokes, drained

To the bowl of a food processor, add the oil, basil, garlic, olives, lemon juice, and Parmesan. Process to a smooth consistency.

Cook the pasta according to package instructions. Drain and immediately toss with the black olive pistou, half of the pieces of chicken, and artichokes. Divide among four plates. Add the rest of the chicken on top if you would like big servings, or save to make sandwiches the next day. Slice the 8 basil leaves thinly and garnish each plate before serving. This salad can be refrigerated and served cold as well.

Cours Saleya Crudités Salad
La Salade de Crudités Cours Saleya

Visitors to the South of France flock to the beach to soak in the sun. Reluctant to leave its warmth in search of lunch or dinner, they dine at the beach restaurants, which have good music and better views. Meanwhile, shoppers in town seek shelter from the summer sun, wedging themselves into small bistros for a cool retreat. Most pick *la formule*, the daily fixed-price menu, which usually includes two or more courses. Vegetarians and those watching their weight eye the *salades composées* on the á la carte menu, one of the most traditional being a *salade de crudités*, which is composed of dressed raw vegetables.

The raw vegetables are usually served three or more to a plate, sometimes arranged on top of a layer of sliced tomatoes. Salads can be made of beets, celery root, cucumber, or carrots, and topped with hard-boiled eggs, olives, or anchovies. Some of the best in Nice are found around the Cours Saleya, in the restaurants that ring the open-air fruit and vegetable market.

It sounds like a lot of work, but these three salads can be made very quickly. Chill them, then arrange on individual plates in three side-by-side rows.

Serves 4

ZUCCHINI SALAD

1/2 teaspoon Dijon mustard

1/4 cup extra virgin olive oil

3 teaspoons red wine vinegar

1/4 teaspoon salt

2 medium zucchini, coarsely grated

8 basil leaves, chopped

12 cherry tomatoes, chopped

Place the mustard in a small bowl and slowly whisk in all the oil. Add the vinegar and salt; whisk.

Toss the zucchini, basil, and tomatoes in the vinaigrette.

MUSHROOM SALAD

1/4 teaspoon Dijon mustard

1/4 cup extra virgin olive oil

3 tablespoons fresh lemon juice

2 anchovies in oil, mashed with a fork

1 small clove garlic, minced

1 pound fresh mushrooms, sliced

In the bottom of a small bowl, place the mustard and slowly whisk in all the oil. Add the lemon juice, anchovies, and garlic; whisk to blend.

Toss mushrooms in the dressing to coat.

CARROT SALAD

1/2 lemon, zested and juiced

1/4 cup extra virgin olive oil

1/4 teaspoon salt

7 medium carrots, peeled

Whisk together 2 tablespoons lemon juice, zest, olive oil, and salt to make a dressing.

Grate the carrots on a box or flat grater, add to a bowl, pour the dressing over the top, and toss to coat.

GRILLED SWORDFISH SALAD
La Salade d'Espadon Grillé

Curls of smoke rose to the terrace, an enticing aroma of crushed pine needles and seared fish. On the table sat the head of a swordfish, its enormous "sword" reaching for the sky.

Our new Australian boat friend Dave had brought us swordfish one Sunday. We were told to relax and make a salad while he took care of setting the table and cooking the fish. Setting the table seemed an odd request, considering he had put the whole head of the fish right in the middle of our outdoor dining table. I was sort of worried this was the centerpiece.

Soon he whisked away the fish head, washed down the table, took the tablecloth from my hands, and proceeded to open and close cupboards in my kitchen, pulling out china and crystal. He found some china decorated with sailors' knots, fish knives I had bought at the Nice antiques market, taffeta blue tall glasses blown in Biot, and my collection of little salt and pepper cellars. The artistic table setting he created took my breath away, and I gasped when I ate his fish. The smell of crushed pine needles had come from the fresh rosemary he laid over the coals in the barbeque and it had scented the fish.

"Where did you learn how to do all of this?" I asked. "It's a beautiful table setting and the fish is divine!"

"I gave up a successful interior decorating business in Sydney to sail the world and do what I love, which is to be on the sea and travel."

As Dave drove out of the driveway, I gasped one last time: sitting in the passenger seat was the swordfish head, apparently on its way to another fishy event.

Serves 4

4 (6-ounce) swordfish steaks

8 tablespoons extra virgin
 olive oil, divided

4 cloves garlic, minced

2 tablespoons fresh lemon juice

1/4 teaspoon fine sea salt

 freshly ground black pepper

4 handfuls of mesclun greens

16 cherry tomatoes, halved

12 fresh basil leaves

4 stalks fresh flat leaf parsley

Heat a griddle pan or barbecue grill until very hot. If you have fresh rosemary, throw a bunch over the barbecue coals.

Coat the swordfish steaks completely using 4 tablespoons olive oil. Sear each side of the steaks on the grill pan or barbecue until done to your liking.

Whisk together the remaining olive oil, garlic, lemon juice, salt, and pepper to taste, and toss the greens and tomatoes with the dressing.

Divide the salad among four plates, flake the grilled swordfish over the top, and garnish with freshly torn basil and parsley leaves.

COMPOSED SALAD VS. SIMPLE SALAD

Salades composées are artfully arranged or layered, such as a Salade Niçoise or vegetables crudités. They can be designed to be a main course, with a layer of greens on each plate, and raw and cooked vegetables and meats, poultry, or seafood laid on top in an appealing way. They are a handy way of using up leftovers and any vegetables and greens you have on hand, resulting in a symphony of colors and flavors and a nourishing meal.

In contrast, simple salads are well mixed or tossed many times with a dressing, presented as a side dish or as the course before serving cheese or dessert. Whether using one ingredient or multiple ingredients, all are placed in a bowl and mixed well with a vinaigrette or sauce.

A BOUQUET OF BROCCOLI
Un Bouquet de Brocoli

My father was an extraordinary and enthusiastic cook, making us everything from Japanese tempura to crêpes suzette to German sauerbraten. He would constantly emerge from the kitchen on weekends with a spoon filled with one of his experiments, asking for our tasting opinion.

This salad was something he created when I was quite young, which I have adopted. He used to call it a bouquet of broccoli. He would be happy to know that his salad would fit perfectly into the style of cooking I was learning years later in the South of France.

Buy as large a broccoli as you can find, then when you get home look for a bowl into which the whole broccoli head will fit snugly.

Serves 4

1 large broccoli

5 tablespoons extra virgin olive oil

1 tablespoon sherry or white wine vinegar

1/2 tablespoon fresh lemon juice

1/2 teaspoon sea salt

1 teaspoon Dijon mustard

1 large shallot, minced

Cut the stalk of the broccoli to about 2 inches long and trim it with a vegetable peeler.

Prepare an ice water bath in a large bowl.

Into salted boiling water, lower the entire broccoli and cook for about 8 to 10 minutes, until the stalk is tender. Remove the broccoli and immediately plunge it into the ice water bath to stop it from cooking and to preserve its color.

Pat the broccoli dry and carefully slice the main stalks so that you can re-construct the broccoli in a bowl to look whole again. For 4 servings, you could slice the broccoli into fourths.

Whisk together the olive oil, vinegar, lemon juice, salt, mustard, and shallot until well combined. Taste and adjust seasonings.

Fit the broccoli into the bowl so it forms a dome, trimming where needed. Pour the vinaigrette over the top and present it with a serving fork to pull the individual pieces out of the bouquet.

NIÇOISE RICE SALAD
La Salade de Riz à la Niçoise

We worked from home and my husband, a former investment banker, was now a pretty fantastic photographer specializing in sailboat races and super-yachts. He chose to leave a profession he was good at for one he loved.

So a lot of our friends in the South of France in the beginning were from the boating industry—captains, stewards, chefs, stewardesses—and we had a steady stream of boat people driving up from Antibes, where most of the boats were docked, to our house for dinner. I often asked them to come and relax on their day off, get comfortable, and help me make dinner.

One late afternoon a couple of girls showed up with supplies. One had been brought up in Nice and wanted to make her mother's rice salad for everyone that evening. It was a snap to make, taking just minutes. It so perfectly captured the essence of summer that I was happy to write down this recipe. It is best served right after making.

Serves 6

4 cups cooked rice

1 large tomato, finely chopped

1 large green bell pepper, finely chopped

1 large orange or yellow bell pepper, finely chopped

2 scallions, thinly sliced

1/2 cup flat leaf parsley, finely chopped

1/2 cup basil leaves, finely chopped

2 (5-ounce) cans light tuna in olive oil

4 tablespoons capers

1 (15 1/4-ounce) can sweet corn nibs, drained

FOR THE VINAIGRETTE

4 tablespoons extra virgin olive oil

3 tablespoons red wine vinegar

1 tablespoon fresh lemon juice

3 teaspoons Dijon mustard

2 cloves garlic, minced

1/2 teaspoon fine sea salt

freshly ground black pepper

In a large serving bowl, add the rice, tomatoes, peppers, scallions, parsley, basil, tuna with its oil from the can, capers, and corn. Combine with a fork.

Whisk together the oil, vinegar, lemon juice, mustard, garlic, salt, and pepper to taste. Pour over the rice mixture, mix well with a fork, and serve.

ROMAINE LETTUCE WITH TUNA CAPER DRESSING
Laitue Romaine, Sauce Mayonnaise de Thon et Câpres

The day the cappuccino-maker-of-my-dreams broke was the day we took a road trip to Genoa. We had been looking for an excuse to make the 2½-hour drive to Italy for lunch, and the cappuccino machine manufacturer informed us we could take it to Genoa for service. So off we went.

On the way, we stopped at a gas station perched on a cliff overlooking the sea and had simply amazing pastries and coffee at their little bar inside the station. And what a view!

On the way home, we stopped at a small restaurant for a light meal and had a mouthwatering *vitello tonnato* — cold, thinly sliced veal frosted with a cool mayonnaise made with tuna and anchovies. The sauce was so beguiling that later in the week I made a *tonnato* sauce for the first time, using it as a salad dressing. I've been serving it this way ever since.

Serves 4

1 tablespoon capers

2 cloves garlic, sliced in thirds

1 tablespoon fresh lemon juice

3 tablespoons red wine vinegar

½ cup mayonnaise

1 (5-ounce) can light tuna in olive oil, best quality

5 anchovies

¼ cup extra virgin olive oil

2 heads romaine lettuce, torn into pieces

Process all of the ingredients, except the lettuce, in a food processor until well blended and smooth.

Pour three-fourths of the dressing over the salad, and toss until evenly coated. Add more dressing if needed.

HERBES DE NICE SALAD
La Salade aux Herbes à la Niçoise

In the hills above Nice, where strawberries, tomatoes, mesclun, and herbs are grown, salads are often a mixture of mesclun and herbs from the garden, supplemented with wild herbs that grow in the area. The herbs most frequently used are basil, fennel, thyme, rosemary, summer savory, hyssop, and marjoram. Foraged wild herbs might include wild thyme, poppy, sow-thistle, and wild marjoram, which is the same as oregano.

So I gave a name to this blend of fresh herbs I found over and over in Niçoise cooking: herbes de Nice. I giggled as I wrote those words for the first time across a gift tag attached to a lovely bunch of them tied with a string, thinking to myself, *Yes, and now I am awarding you a much-deserved appellation*, addressing the herbs in front of me as if they could hear what I was saying. *As guardian of the geographical boundaries of my herb garden, I hereby grant you the appellation, herbes de Nice!*

And what an inspired blend. I love it so much that I planted rows of the herbs that make up the classic Niçoise mix side by side in my garden, so that I could sweep in and gather them for my cooking or gifting.

You can replicate herbes de Nice by planting a windowsill garden, which requires only that you buy plants and nurture them in a sunny window: oregano, basil, thyme, rosemary, and marjoram. The fennel herb grows to be quite large, but you could grow it if you have a garden and add it to the herbes de Nice blend.

Serves 4

10 oregano leaves

12 basil leaves (reserve 6 whole)

5 thyme sprigs, leaves only

5 rosemary needles

20 marjoram leaves (reserve 10 whole)

4 tablespoons coarsely chopped fennel fronds (from the fennel bulb below)

8 cups mesclun, or a mix of whatever salad greens you have

1/2 small fennel bulb, very thinly sliced

1/4 cup extra virgin olive oil, divided

3 teaspoons red wine vinegar

1/4 teaspoon Dijon mustard

1/4 teaspoon salt

Stem and wash the herbs and dry on paper towels. Save 6 basil leaves and 10 marjoram leaves to put into the salad whole. Gather all remaining herbs, including the fennel frond, into a compact bundle, and with a sharp knife, cut into thin slices; then rock the blade over the herbs to chop them very finely. This will be your herbes de Nice.

Place the salad leaves in a large bowl, add the sliced fennel, tear in the 6 leaves of basil, add the whole marjoram leaves, and scatter the herbes de Nice over the top. Add half the olive oil and toss well to coat. Add more if needed.

Whisk together the vinegar, mustard, and salt. Drizzle over the salad and toss well to coat.

LATE-AUGUST DOUBLE FIG SALAD WITH ARUGULA, GOAT CHEESE AND HAZELNUTS

La Salade de Fin Août aux Fiques Deux Façons avec Roquette, Fromage de Chèvre et Noisettes

There were over fifty jars of freshly made fig jam surrounding me as I sat cross-legged on the kitchen floor, counting them. I was struck by the thought of how different my life was from when I worked at a bank in London, at the center of a fast-paced industry in a fast-paced city, having now given up high heels for canvas espadrilles. I was working at home with my husband, at a much slower pace, in a country I loved, finding time to make jam from the figs growing around our house.

In late August, when my fig trees were pregnant with red, green, and black figs, I felt compelled to rush out and use them up before they fell. Rather than letting them fall and be smashed in the driveway, I would gather them and carry basketsful into my kitchen to simmer into jams and preserves. There were four monolithic towering trees with arms reaching out nearly as wide as their height, and they produced prodigiously. As soon as I made jam, the next day there would be more fresh figs. This salad is one of the ways I found to use them.

Serves 4

1	tablespoon extra virgin olive oil
16	fresh figs, stems removed, divided
3	tablespoons honey
2	teaspoons red wine vinegar
1/8	teaspoon anise extract
1/4	cup extra virgin olive oil
1	tablespoon sherry or white wine vinegar
1	teaspoon fresh thyme leaves
1	tablespoon raisins
	salt
	freshly ground black pepper
4	cups arugula leaves
2	ounces fresh goat cheese, room temperature
4	tablespoons roasted hazelnuts, coarsely chopped

Preheat oven to 350 degrees F. Lightly oil a shallow baking or gratin dish.

Slice 8 of the figs in half vertically and arrange in the baking dish cut side up. Whisk together the honey, red wine vinegar, and anise extract, then spoon a little over each fig half. Place in the oven and cook for 15 minutes. Remove and allow to cool to room temperature.

Slice the other 8 figs in half vertically. In a food processor, process the olive oil, vinegar, thyme, and raisins. Taste and add salt and freshly ground black pepper if desired.

Toss the arugula with the dressing and divide among four plates. Arrange 2 halves of the baked figs and 2 halves of fresh figs on each salad. Shower each plate with crumbled goat cheese and 1 tablespoon hazelnuts.

Orange, Black Olive, and Gorgonzola Salad

La Salade aux Oranges et Olives Noires à la Gorgonzola

One night I made sashimi and sushi, Italian style. And a salad, Japanese style. For the sushi, I speared a scallop with a fork and then twirled it in pasta to make little "sushi" rolls. For the salad, I sliced the orange like sashimi, thin and square. Served with candlelight and a bit of humor, it was the salad that stuck.

Serves 4

24 oil-cured black olives, divided

4 tablespoons extra virgin olive oil

1 tablespoon sherry or white balsamic vinegar

1 tablespoon water

1 teaspoon Dijon mustard

4 oranges

4 cups mesclun or other mixed green leaves

4 ounces Gorgonzola cheese

fleur de sel

Pit 16 of the olives and slice into halves or quarters. Reserve for garnish.

Pit 8 olives and pulse in a food processor until chopped.

In a bowl, make a vinaigrette by whisking the olive oil, vinegar, water, and mustard until well blended, then whisk in the 8 chopped olives.

Slice the peel from the oranges down to the flesh. Slice the oranges into even rounds, then trim into squares.

To serve, toss the salad greens in the vinaigrette and divide among individual plates. Arrange the square orange slices on top in a line, sashimi style. Crumble Gorgonzola cheese over the top and garnish with the 16 sliced olives. Sprinkle a little fleur de sel over the top of the oranges before serving.

PASTAS, RISOTTO, PIZZAS

Les Pâtes, Les Risottos, Les Pizzas

FOOD PROCESSOR FRESH PASTA
Les Pâtes Fraîches de Robot Culinaire

The love of pasta in the area around Nice has reached such proportions that Niçoise versions, such as ravioli stuffed with Swiss chard and cheese, are offered on menus next to Italian pasta dishes—greatly expanding a pasta lover's choices. Pissaladière joins flavorful crisp pizza of all kinds. Fresh spinach noodles sauced with Nice's pistou are offered alongside Genoa's version made with pesto, while Merda de Can, an ancient Niçoise dish, is listed alongside Italian-style gnocchi.

Inspired by this, I began trying every pasta recipe that looked interesting. I had already securely fastened my hand-cranked pasta machine with screws to a counter in my kitchen and made great sheets of fresh dough, which I cut into ribbons and draped over every available chair back in the house so they could dry until I was finished making a batch and could cook them. Someday, I told myself, I would drive into Italy, where I was sure to find some sort of wooden structure on which to more formally hang my pasta.

Using a food processor is the quickest and easiest way to make pasta. It takes literally seconds to prepare and produces a pasta that will melt in your mouth it is so tender. Use a pasta machine to roll out the dough and cut it. If you don't have one, roll out the dough as thinly as you can with a rolling pin and cut with a sharp knife or pizza cutter into the shapes you want.

When you are ready to cook the pasta, use a large pot so the pasta has room to move around in the water. Bring water to a boil, salt it generously, then drop in the homemade pasta and cook for only 30 seconds, or until it is tender but still has a bite to it. Carefully drain, then add it to the sauce you are using.

Serves 4

2 large eggs

4 large egg yolks

2 teaspoons extra virgin olive oil

¼ teaspoon salt

2 cups flour

Whisk the eggs, yolks, olive oil, and salt together, then pour into the bowl of a food processor.

Add the flour and process. If a ball forms, fine; stop there. If not and you have fine pearls, that's okay too. Just scoop them out onto a piece of parchment paper and bring the dough together into a ball with your hands. Knead three or four times.

If the dough feels wet, add 1 tablespoon more of flour and knead it into the dough ball. Eggs vary in how liquid they are and in how much flour they can absorb, so start with the lesser amount, test with your finger, and add more if it seems sticky. Wrap the dough ball in plastic wrap and allow it to rest for 30 to 45 minutes.

Divide the dough ball into six pieces, working with one and covering the others. Roll out, one by one, through the pasta machine. When you reach the #5 position, you may want to slice the sheet of dough in half if it has become too long. I roll my pasta to the #8 position, or very thinly, before feeding it through the cutters.

If you are working by hand, roll out the dough as thinly as you can with a rolling pin, then cut the dough into pasta with a sharp knife or pizza cutter. Either way, use no extra flour or as little as possible, since adding flour will make the pasta a bit gooey when cooked.

Hang the pasta as you cut it on the backs of chairs covered with clean towels. When it is all done, drop into boiling water to cook. Depending on how thinly you rolled your dough and what width of pasta you cut, it could take from 30 seconds to 2 minutes to cook; so stand nearby and test a strand to see when it gets to a good place for you. Drain, toss with sauce, and serve.

Pasta Party with Three Sauces
La Fête de Pâtes avec Trois Sauces

If you're going to make pasta, make a lot. You can freeze any you don't use right away. Or you can have a pasta party. Line up bowls along a counter. Serve a big family-style bowl of pasta, three more bowls of delectable sauces, and smaller bowls filled with mix-and-match toppings, including chopped fresh basil, chopped fresh oregano, and hot pepper flakes. Place a large hunk of Parmesan cheese and a grater at the end of the line, a bowl of dressed salad and warmed bread, and you'll have enough for a crowd to feast on.

Here are three sauces to make for the party. Use the recipe for Food Processor Fresh Pasta on page 101 and double or triple it, depending on how many you are serving. Cook the pasta, then toss it in enough extra virgin olive oil to barely coat, and keep warm until ready to serve.

TOMATO SAUCE WITH ROSÉ WINE

Serves 6

4 tablespoons extra virgin olive oil

1 medium-size yellow onion, finely chopped

5 cloves garlic, finely chopped

1 carrot, grated

1/2 cup rosé wine or chicken broth

3 teaspoons sugar

1/2 teaspoon sea salt

2 teaspoons fresh thyme leaves

1 tablespoon fresh basil, finely chopped

1/2 can tomato paste

1 (28-ounce can) San Marzano whole tomatoes in juice

In a large saucepan, heat the oil and add the onion and garlic. Cook for 3 minutes. Add the rest of the ingredients and simmer for 30 minutes, crushing the tomatoes roughly with a fork. Or, for a silky smooth sauce, put it through a food mill. Pour the sauce into a serving bowl.

PISTOU SAUCE

Serves 6

4 large cloves garlic

6 ounces Parmesan cheese, sliced

2 cups tightly packed fresh basil leaves

1 teaspoon salt

1 cup extra virgin olive oil

Put the garlic, cheese, basil, and salt in a food processor and process for 5 seconds. With the machine running, add the oil in a thin stream until well blended. If you would like a thinner sauce, add more olive oil and blend again. Pour the sauce into a serving bowl.

CLAM AND MUSHROOM SAUCE

Serves 6

9 tablespoons extra virgin olive oil, divided

1/2 medium yellow onion, finely chopped

5 cloves garlic, minced

1 teaspoon thyme leaves

1/2 pound mushrooms, trimmed and finely chopped

1/4 teaspoon sea salt

freshly ground black pepper

1 (15-ounce) can whole baby clams

1 (8-ounce) jar clam juice

5 anchovies, chopped

1 cup dry white wine

2 tablespoons Pernod, optional

2 pounds small clams

4 tablespoons minced flat leaf parsley

In a large skillet, heat 6 tablespoons oil, then add the onion and garlic and cook for 3 minutes. Turn up the heat, add the thyme, mushrooms, salt, and pepper to taste; cook for 5 minutes, stirring constantly.

Pour the can of clams through a fine sieve lined with paper towels or a paper coffee filter, catching the liquid. To the skillet, add the filtered liquid from the canned clams, jarred clam juice, anchovies, white wine, and Pernod, and bring to a simmer.

Scrub the clams, add to the skillet, and cover. Cook just until the shells have opened. Add the canned clams to the broth and heat but do not cook, as they will become rubbery.

Pour the sauce into a serving bowl, and shower with parsley.

EGG NOODLES
Les Nouilles aux Oeufs

Even though winters are mild in Bar-sur-Loup, a sudden strong, chilly wind can sweep down from the mountains, forcing even the weeds to genuflect. One of my first cooking lessons with Madame was on a day like this. As I climbed the hill to her house, it looked like a Christmas card, a golden silhouette with a warmly lit interior against the darkening sky.

I had brought the wooden spoon she gave me as a gift. Its inauguration was to be the process of stirring up delicious bits of browned garlic and onions from the bottom of a cast-iron pot. We made a Niçoise daube and spent the rest of the afternoon spinning out tender egg noodles for it to rest on.

Serves 4-6

1 1/2 cups all-purpose flour, more if needed

1 teaspoon salt

1/8 teaspoon freshly ground black pepper

2 large eggs

2 large egg yolks

1 teaspoon extra virgin olive oil

To the bowl of a food processor, add all the ingredients and process until a ball is formed. Add an extra tablespoon of flour if it seems too wet, and process again until smooth. (We made this by hand, without the aid of a food processor. If you follow our lead, place the flour, salt, and pepper in a heap on a clean work surface. Beat the eggs together with the olive oil, make a well in the center of the flour, pour in the egg mixture, and bring all together with your hands. Knead until you have a nice soft dough. Sprinkle on a little flour if the dough is too wet, then knead. Or add a tablespoon of water if it is too dry, and knead.) Scoop out the dough, wrap it in plastic wrap, and allow to rest for 30 to 45 minutes.

Slice the ball into 6 pieces and roll one at a time through a pasta machine until you have thin sheets, then feed through the cutting attachment for wide noodles; or roll out very thinly with a rolling pin and slice into wide noodle strips. Drop into generously salted boiling water and cook for 30 seconds to 1 minute, until tender. Drain, coat with just enough olive oil to keep the noodles from sticking together, and keep warm until ready to use.

ANGEL HAIR PASTA WITH FRIDAY SAUCE
Les Pâtes Cheveux d'Ange à la Sauce de Vendredi

I saw his black robes again, just turning the corner of the church. This time I followed *le père qui mange* (father who eats) and introduced myself, explaining that I had observed him enjoying chilled mussels one afternoon in the restaurant near the church, and I enjoyed them as well. We began talking about how I had just moved to a house down the road, and about food and how I was collecting recipes from people who lived around me. He offered to give me his favorite, one he makes on meatless Fridays.

The only change I have made to it is adding olives and sometimes a sprinkle of hot pepper flakes. The priest who loved to eat is no longer there, but I like to think he is still making and enjoying this dish on Fridays.

Serves 4

1 pound dried angel hair pasta

¼ cup extra virgin olive oil

1 can anchovies in olive oil

6 cloves garlic, pressed

1 teaspoon fresh lemon juice

2 tablespoons pitted black olives or oil-cured olives, minced

pinch of cayenne pepper

1 cup freshly grated Parmesan cheese

Cook the pasta in a pot of well-salted boiling water according to package instructions. Drain, drizzle with just enough olive oil to coat, and keep warm.

In a large skillet, heat the olive oil, anchovies and their oil from the can, garlic, and lemon juice. Sauté over very low heat until they almost melt and you can mash the anchovies and garlic into a paste with a fork. Whisk to blend well. Stir in the olives and cayenne.

Pour the pasta into the skillet, toss to coat with the anchovy sauce, and sauté for 1 minute.

Divide among four plates and serve with freshly grated Parmesan cheese on top.

SWISS CHARD GNOCCHI
La Merda de Can

Merda de can is an old Niçoise dish of potato gnocchi made with Swiss chard. It is served simply in restaurants in old town Nice with fruity olive oil, salt, lots of coarsely grated black pepper, and freshly grated Parmesan. Delicious this way, and wonderful served as a soft bed for a beef daube, you'll also see it prepared with gorgonzola sauce, the recipe for which follows.

Merda de can and gnocchi come together easily when you make them at home. The trick is to wing it. Do like grandmothers did and make your gnocchi on a clean, lightly floured kitchen counter or table, bringing it together with your hands and "feeling" if more flour is needed to make a pliable dough to work with.

Below you will find the basic starting point for making your merda de can gnocchi. Mine come together with anywhere from 1¹/₂ to 2 cups of flour. So measure out 1 cup in one bowl, then measure out 2 other bowls with ¹/₂ cup flour each to add one at a time, if needed.

The instructions might seem long, but because it is a matter of "feel" rather than science, I want to talk you through it the first time!

Tip: use a potato ricer to achieve the lightest gnocchi possible.

Serves 4

2 large Russet potatoes, scrubbed

2 cups tightly packed Swiss chard, leaves only

1 large egg

$^1/_4$ teaspoon salt

1$^1/_2$–2 cups all-purpose flour

$^1/_2$ cup olive oil

Heat the oven to 375 degrees F.

Pierce the potatoes with a fork in 4 places then bake for 60 minutes. Wearing a kitchen mitt, squeeze potatoes to see if they are soft. If not, bake another 10 minutes. They should be very soft. Remove from the oven, cool, and peel.

Meanwhile, wash the Swiss chard leaves and dry them thoroughly. Drop into a food processor and quickly pulse 7 times to mince. Scoop out onto paper towels and dab with another paper towel to completely dry.

Put the potatoes through a potato ricer onto a clean, lightly floured surface. Fluff with a fork. Beat egg with the salt and pour over the potatoes; mix in with a fork. Scoop the Swiss chard on top. Put 1 cup of the flour in a sieve and shake back and forth over the Swiss chard.

Now use your hands to bring it all together into a dough, kneading with the heel of your hand until the dough forms. If it feels too wet, add another $^1/_2$ cup flour and knead again. If it is still not coming together, add the remaining $^1/_2$ cup flour and knead again. If it is still sticky, sprinkle a little flour over the top and knead again. You are looking for a soft dough that is pliable and doesn't fall apart.

Scrape clean the work surface, lightly flour again, and begin to make the gnocchi. Slice off a piece of dough, roll into a log about 1 inch in diameter, and cut off a 1-inch piece. Cook it in well-salted boiling water until it dances to the top, then cook for a further 2 to 3 minutes, or until tender. If it doesn't fall apart and it tastes good, slice the remaining dough into several pieces, roll them

into long logs about 1 inch in diameter, then cut into 1-inch pieces. If the test gnocchi falls apart, add more flour to the dough and knead again, then roll into logs and slice into 1-inch pieces. Niçoise gnocchi are larger than you are used to seeing. I push mine together from both ends a little bit to make them plump.

As the gnocchi are cooked, remove them with a slotted spoon to a colander to drain; then drizzle with a little olive oil, toss, and keep warm until you sauce them.

Gnocchi will keep in the freezer for 3 months and can be dropped frozen right into a pot of boiling water.

GORGONZOLA SAUCE

6 ounces Gorgonzola cheese, room temperature

$^1/_3$ cup whole milk

$^2/_3$ cup heavy cream

salt

freshly ground black pepper

1 cup freshly grated Parmesan cheese

In a skillet or saucepan big enough to hold all the gnocchi, melt the Gorgonzola in the milk and cream over medium heat, stirring continuously and tasting for seasoning. Add salt and pepper as needed.

Pour in the cooked gnocchi, toss to coat, and heat while stirring for 1 minute. Serve with a separate bowl of freshly grated Parmesan cheese.

RISOTTO WITH PARMESAN, RICOTTA AND LEMON
Le Risotto de Ricotta, Parmigiano Reggiano et Citron

Valbonne Dumanois came highly recommended as one of the best vegetable and fruit stores in the area, something of a destination in itself, with "forgotten" vegetables, huge lemons, tiny strawberries from Carros, ten or more varieties of tomatoes, fresh walnuts in season, wild foraged mushrooms, pears worthy of being painted, and peas that would burst in your mouth with sugary sweetness.

It was where you would bump into others impatiently in search of the first asparagus of spring and the plumpest, sweetest Muscat grapes. The desire to eat well sparked conversations amongst strangers in its aisles, trading information about how to prepare recipes using what they were finding in the store or about which chefs were cooking the best dishes of the season. I can't count the number of recipe suggestions I received simply from shopping there, including this one for a lemony risotto.

Serves 4

6 cups chicken broth

7 tablespoons extra virgin olive oil, divided

1/2 cup finely minced onion

2 cups Arborio or risotto rice

1 cup dry vermouth or white wine

1 tablespoon fresh thyme leaves, minced

1 large lemon, zested and juiced

2 cups freshly grated Parmesan, divided

salt

freshly grated black pepper

1 cup whole milk ricotta cheese

Heat the chicken broth in a saucepan and keep it simmering until ready to use.

Heat 5 tablespoons olive oil in a large skillet, add the onion, and cook on low heat for about 3 minutes, until soft and translucent.

Turn the heat up to medium and add the rice, cooking and stirring it with a wooden spoon until it looks translucent. Add the vermouth or wine and keep stirring until it has evaporated.

Add 1 cup of the hot chicken broth to the rice and continue stirring until the rice has absorbed the liquid. Add the next cup and stir until absorbed. Repeat, stirring continuously, until all the broth has been used. The risotto should be creamy and still a bit wet. If the rice is dry and needs to cook longer, add extra water and cook until it is creamy.

At the end, stir in 2 tablespoons olive oil, thyme, half of the lemon zest, lemon juice, 1 cup Parmesan cheese, and salt and pepper to taste. Then gently fold in the ricotta cheese until just blended.

Ladle the risotto onto serving plates, sprinkle with the remaining lemon zest, and serve immediately with remaining Parmesan cheese on the side.

Note: Salmon, grilled shrimp, scallops, and lobster are all tasty additions, as are fresh peas in the spring.

Valbonne Dumanois
4 Place Vignasse 06560 Valbonne
Telephone: (33) 04 93 12 08 28

NIÇOISE MACARONI
Les Macaronis à la Niçoise

"I like all simple things; boiled eggs, oysters and caviar, *truite au bleu*, grilled salmon, roast lamb, cold grouse, treacle tart and rice pudding. But of all simple things the only one I can eat day in day out, not only without disgust but with the eagerness of an appetite unimpaired by excess, is macaroni."
—from the short story *The Hairless Mexican*, by Somerset Maugham, who lived near Nice on Cap Ferrat for forty years

Serves 4

1 pound macaroni

6 tablespoons olive oil

1 small onion, chopped

3 cloves garlic, chopped

4 anchovies

4 cups tomatoes, finely chopped

1 teaspoon sugar

1/4 teaspoon sea salt

freshly ground black pepper

1/2 cup oil-cured black olives, pitted and sliced

1 1/2 cups Parmesan cheese, divided

1/4 cup finely chopped fresh basil

Cook the macaroni according to package instructions, then drain.

In a large skillet, heat the olive oil over medium heat, add the onion, garlic, and anchovies, and cook just until the garlic begins to turn golden, about 3 minutes. Add the tomatoes, sugar, salt, and pepper to taste. Lower the heat and cook for another 3 minutes, stirring constantly.

Add the macaroni, olives, 1/2 cup Parmesan, and basil to the sauce in the skillet, and stir to combine.

Serve with a drizzle of olive oil over the top and with the remaining Parmesan in a bowl on the side.

GOAT CHEESE RAVIOLI WITH WILD MUSHROOMS
Les Raviolis au Fromage de Chèvre et Ricotta avec Champignons Sauvages

Soft brown and bright orange wild mushrooms piled in glorious abundance on top of the ravioli released a primal aroma into the air. The dish before me was a revelation, a poignant pairing of produce plucked from damp woods and cheese made with milk coaxed from goats grazing in a field.

After tasting this dish in a famous restaurant nearby, I wanted to make it. Whether I could ever succeed in replicating it would be another matter. I tried and I tried. And what became clear in the process was that if you use the very best quality of everything that goes into it, you can come pretty close. Close enough to make at least a superb dish.

Serves 4

1 recipe Food Processor Fresh Pasta (page 101)

¼ cup boiling water

2 tablespoons raisins

8 ounces goat cheese, room temperature

8 ounces whole milk ricotta

½ teaspoon sea salt, divided

6 tablespoons extra virgin olive oil

2 cloves garlic, minced

coarsely ground black pepper

1 pound mixed wild mushrooms, halved or quartered

1 cup freshly grated Parmesan cheese

Roll out pasta dough in your machine to the second thinnest setting, then cut into 6 sheets measuring 12 x 12 inches. Cover with a towel. Line a baking sheet with parchment paper.

Pour the water over the raisins and allow to sit until plump; drain and coarsely chop. Scoop raisins into a mixing bowl, add the goat cheese, ricotta, ¼ teaspoon salt, and mix well. Taste and add more salt if needed.

Place one pasta sheet in front of you horizontally on a clean work surface. Place another sheet just above it, and cover the remaining sheets with a kitchen towel.

Put tablespoons of filling with spaces in between on one sheet. Lightly moisten the dough around the filling with water, then place the other rectangle of dough on top. Use your fingers to press down around the mounds of filling so there are no air pockets. Slice into ravioli squares or circles, or use a cookie cutter or small glass as a guide to cut shapes. Press the edges once again firmly with your fingers to seal. Place on baking sheet until ready to use.

Bring a large pot of generously salted water to a gentle boil, then lower the raviolis into the water. Reduce to a simmer and cook for 3 to 4 minutes. When raviolis float to the top, they are done. With a slotted spoon, gently lift the raviolis out of the water and drain in a colander.

Warm the olive oil, garlic, ¼ teaspoon salt, and pepper to taste over medium heat for 3 minutes. Add the mushrooms, and gently turn them with a spoon to coat and warm.

Place the raviolis on plates, drizzle with a little olive oil, top with the mushrooms, and serve with grated Parmesan.

SAVORY RICE PUDDING WITH SPINACH AND PARMESAN
Fada Riquet

One of the dishes that I tried from Mireille Johnston's *The Cuisine of the Sun* was something I have never seen offered on a restaurant menu; yet I knew it must be Niçoise, as she was born in Nice and grew up there. She calls it Fada Riquet. A comforting food I often turn to, it is a bit like creamed spinach, with rice and cheese, and makes a substantial meal. This is an adaptation of Johnston's original recipe.

Serves 4

2   cups chicken stock

³/₄ cup rice

3   (10-ounce) packages frozen chopped spinach, thawed

1   cup milk

¹/₂ teaspoon sea salt

    freshly ground black pepper

    dash of cayenne pepper

3   eggs, beaten

1³/₄ cups freshly grated Parmesan cheese, divided

2   tablespoons olive oil

2   teaspoons fresh thyme leaves

Place the chicken stock and rice in a large saucepan and bring to a boil; reduce the heat, cover, and cook for 15 minutes. Add the spinach and cook on medium heat for another 5 minutes, stirring frequently.

Add the milk, salt, lots of black pepper, and cayenne; cook on medium heat for 4 minutes.

Off the heat, vigorously stir in the eggs and ³/₄ cup grated cheese until well combined. Place back on the heat and cook over low heat, stirring frequently, for 4 minutes. Add the olive oil, thyme, and salt and pepper to taste; stir to combine. Serve with the remaining cheese in a bowl on the side.

PISSALADIÈRE
La Pissaladière

Another snack sold everywhere in Nice is the Niçoise pizza called *pissaladière*, which has a topping of onions, olives, and anchovies and is normally sliced into large squares.

It takes very little time to make the dough in a food processor. If you don't have time to make it, your local pizza restaurant will sell you a fresh ball of dough.

Tip: Place the whole onions in the freezer for 15 minutes before slicing to reduce tearing.

Makes 8 medium-size squares or 16 small squares

FOR THE DOUGH

2 1/4 cups all-purpose flour or bread flour

1 teaspoon fine sea salt

3/4 cup warm water

1 packet (2 1/4 teaspoons) active dry yeast

1 teaspoon sugar

1/8 cup warm milk

1 egg, beaten

1 teaspoon garlic, minced

2 tablespoons extra virgin olive oil

FOR THE TOPPING

6 tablespoons extra virgin olive oil

5 medium sweet white onions (e.g., Vidalia)

1 (2-ounce) can anchovies in oil, drained

3 cloves garlic, minced

1/4 teaspoon fine sea salt

2 teaspoons sugar, divided

1/2 teaspoon freshly ground black pepper

1 tablespoon fresh thyme leaves

20 pitted Niçoise olives, or very good quality black olives, pitted and halved

To make the dough, place the flour and salt in the bowl of a food processor. (If you have a plastic dough blade, use it.)

Pour the warm water into a small bowl, sprinkle the yeast over the top, stir in sugar, and let stand for 8 minutes, until foamy.

With the food processor running, pour the yeast mixture, milk, and egg through the tube, and process until the dough comes together in a ball. Add the garlic and oil and process again for a couple of seconds.

Scoop out the dough ball, place in an oiled bowl, cover with plastic wrap then a towel, and set in a warm place to rise for 1 1/2 hours.

Preheat the oven to 425 degrees F.

Slice the onions in half, then slice very thinly.

Mince 10 of the anchovy fillets. Slice the rest of the anchovies into four pieces.

You will be cooking two batches at once because it is a lot of onions to fit into one skillet. Divide the olive oil between two large skillets and heat. Divide the onions and garlic equally between the two skillets. Cook on low heat, stirring frequently, until the onions are very soft, about 45 minutes. Add the salt, half the sugar, pepper, minced anchovies, and thyme leaves to each skillet; stir and cook for 5 minutes. Then allow the mixture to cool to room temperature.

Liberally oil a 12 x 17-inch baking sheet with olive oil. With a rolling pin, roll out the dough on a clean floured work surface to the size of the baking sheet, then place the dough onto the sheet, using your fingers to spread it to the edges.

Spread the onion mixture evenly on top, scatter the remaining anchovy pieces and the olives on top, and bake the pissaladière for about 20 to 25 minutes, or until golden.

Remove from the oven and, after 5 minutes, slice the pissaladière in half vertically, then in half horizontally, and twice again vertically to yield 8 pieces. For small squares, slice the 8 pieces in half, then in half again.

Menton Tomato and Onion Pizza
La Pichade de Menton

One of the prettiest towns on the coast, blessed with a front-row seat facing the Mediterranean Sea and circled by orange and lemon groves, Menton is a constant delight to visit.

At one end of the culinary spectrum, it is home to the Michelin two-star restaurant Mirazur, where one of the most exciting chefs in France, Mauro Colagreco, is creating delicate modern food inspired by what is around him—vegetables and herbs from his kitchen garden, fish brought to him from the old port just down the road, and produce from nearby hills and valleys. On the other end of the spectrum, Menton celebrates its ancient French-Italian culinary heritage in many of its other restaurants, food stalls in the open-air markets, and at town fairs. The *pichade de Menton* is one of their traditional dishes. A sturdy rectangular pizza that looks a bit like pissaladière, it is bright red, decorated with green and black olives and flat leaf parsley. Once made, the pizza can be sliced into squares and eaten at room temperature or packed for a picnic or road trip. Make sure to cook it in a very hot oven and on a pizza stone if you have one, preheating the oven with the stone in it for at least 40 minutes before placing the pizza on it.

Makes 8 medium-size squares or 16 small squares

FOR THE DOUGH

2 1/4 cups all-purpose flour or bread flour

1 teaspoon fine sea salt

3/4 cup warm water

1 package (2 1/4 teaspoons) active dry yeast

1 teaspoon sugar

1/8 cup warm milk

1 egg, beaten

1 teaspoon garlic, minced

2 tablespoons extra virgin olive oil

FOR THE TOPPING

5 medium-size sweet white onions (e.g., Vidalia)

5 medium-size tomatoes

1 (2-ounce) can anchovies in oil, drained

6 tablespoons extra virgin olive oil

3 cloves garlic, minced

1/4 teaspoon fine sea salt

2 teaspoons sugar

1/2 teaspoon freshly ground black pepper

20 pitted Niçoise olives, or very good quality black and green olives, pitted and halved

1 cup flat leaf parsley, leaves only, chopped

To make the dough, place the flour and salt in the bowl of a food processor. (If you have a plastic dough blade, use it.)

Pour the warm water into a small bowl, sprinkle the yeast over the top, stir in the sugar, and let stand for 8 minutes, until foamy.

With the machine running, pour the yeast mixture, milk, and egg through the feed tube and process until the dough comes together in a ball. Add the garlic and the oil and process again for a couple of seconds.

Scoop out the dough ball, place in an oiled bowl, cover with plastic wrap then a towel, and set in a warm place to rise for 1 1/2 hours.

Preheat the oven to 425 degrees F. Fill a large bowl with water and some ice cubes.

To prepare the topping, slice the onions in half, then slice very thinly. Set aside.

Blanch the tomatoes in boiling water, counting to 10, then drain and drop tomatoes into the ice water bath. When cool, peel and chop coarsely.

Mince 10 of the anchovy fillets. Slice the rest of the anchovies into four pieces.

You will be cooking two batches at once because it is a lot of onions and tomatoes to fit into one skillet. Divide the olive oil between two large skillets and heat. Divide the onion, tomatoes, and garlic evenly between the two skillets. Cook on low heat, stirring frequently, until the onions and tomatoes are very soft, about 45 minutes. Add the salt and half each of the sugar, pepper, and minced anchovies to each skillet; stir and cook for 5 minutes. Then allow the mixture to cool to room temperature.

To make the pizza, liberally oil a 12 x 17-inch baking sheet with olive oil. With a rolling pin, roll out the dough on a clean, floured work surface to the size of the baking sheet, then place the dough on the sheet. Using your fingers, spread the dough to the edges.

Evenly spread the onion-tomato mixture on top, scatter the remaining anchovy pieces and the olives on top, paint some olive oil on the crust with a pastry brush, and bake for about 20 to 25 minutes, or until golden. Scatter the parsley over the top, slice, and serve.

VEGETABLE GARDEN PIZZA
La Pizza du Potager

Madame up the hill moved about her garden as a butterfly would, hovering here, flitting there, touching down briefly to smell or snip. Old bones walked with lightness, gliding through long rows of vegetables, making her work look easy.

I'd rest my chin on the railing of her fence and watch her silently before she would notice I was there. Suddenly radiant and full of excitement, she'd reach for a wicker basket at her feet and walk in my direction. Whatever was in it was to be mine. It could be filled with zucchini. And certainly with celery, as Monsieur seemed to plant acres of it.

Between us we had a wealth of vegetables and fruits we shared with the delight felt by good friends being able to give endless gifts to one another. When my tomatoes and her zucchini came together in a pizza, it seemed an anthem to our kindred love for our gardens.

Makes 1 pizza

1 packet (2¼ teaspoons) active dry yeast

⅞ cup warm water

4 tablespoon extra virgin olive oil, divided

2¼ cups all-purpose flour, plus ¼ cup extra

1½ teaspoons sea salt, divided

⅛ teaspoon freshly ground black pepper

2 tablespoons minced fresh marjoram leaves, plus 3 tablespoons whole leaves

2 large tomatoes, yellow or red, thinly sliced

1 zucchini, yellow or green, very thinly sliced

1 small red, yellow, or green bell pepper, chopped

1 small white onion, finely chopped

1½ cups whole milk ricotta cheese

Dissolve the yeast in the warm water for 15 minutes. Then add 1 tablespoon olive oil to the yeast water and stir.

Meanwhile, put the 2¼ cups flour, 1 teaspoon salt, pepper, and minced marjoram leaves in the bowl of a food processor.

With the food processor running, pour the yeast-water mixture through the feed tube and run until a dough ball forms. Add more flour if necessary to make a smooth, soft dough ball. Scoop out the dough into an oiled bowl, cover, and let rise for 2 hours.

Preheat the oven to 450 degrees F.

Push the dough down with your knuckles, then transfer it to a lightly floured work surface. With a floured rolling pin, roll out the dough, starting from the center and working out to the edges all the way around. Turn over and repeat on the other side, until it reaches the thickness and size you would like. No need to be perfect; the pizza looks rustic if randomly shaped.

Transfer to an oiled pizza pan or baking sheet. Lightly brush the pizza dough with extra virgin olive oil. Arrange the tomato slices over the pizza, then the zucchini, bell pepper, and onion. Scatter the whole marjoram leaves over the top. Drizzle the top with remaining 3 tablespoons olive oil and season with remaining ½ teaspoon salt. Drop spoonfuls of ricotta cheese decoratively across the pizza.

Bake for 15 to 20 minutes, until golden.

Note: If you like a thicker crust, allow the pizza to stand with its toppings for 20 minutes before baking.

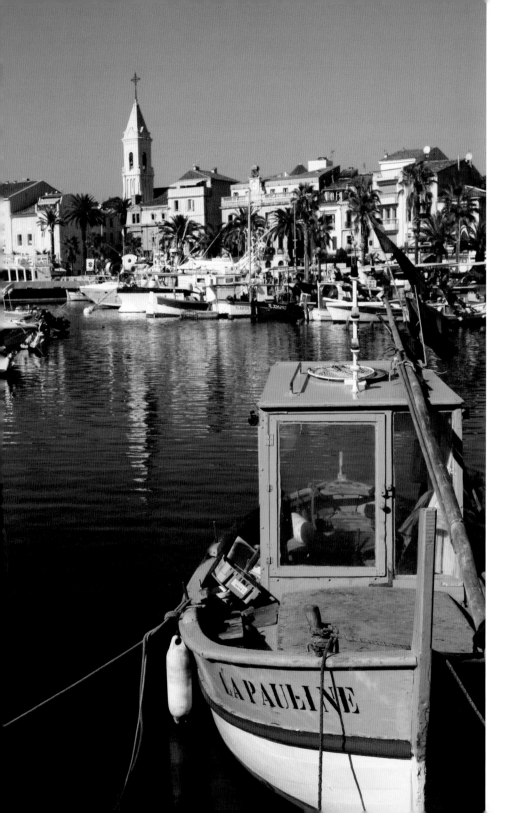

PIZZA FROM THE SEA
La Pizza de la Mer

The siren of Nice unbraided her long blond hair and let it float on the breeze. Neptune rose from the sea, sitting at a table made of sea shells, and beckoned her to join him. She drifted over, settled gently on a soft cushion beside him, and took to her lips the bite of food he offered.

Or so I imagined. I was waiting for my pizza at a restaurant by the port and could hear seagulls with a French accent calling out impatiently to the waiter to hurry with my order and their crumbs. He arrived. Not quite Neptune, but once I tasted the pizza from the sea that he gave me, I slipped back into my dream. I unbraided my hair and let if float on the breeze.

Makes 1 pizza

7/8 cup warm water

1 packet (2 1/4 teaspoons) active dry yeast

7 tablespoon extra virgin olive oil, divided, plus extra to drizzle

2 1/4 cups all-purpose flour, plus 1/4 cup extra

1 1/2 teaspoons sea salt, divided

2 cups tightly packed basil leaves, plus 6 leaves reserved

3 cloves garlic, minced

1/4 cup grated Parmesan cheese

2 (6-ounce) cans premium-quality light tuna in olive oil, drained

14 fresh medium shrimp, peeled, deveined, and halved vertically

1/4 cup chopped red bell pepper

1/4 cup chopped yellow bell pepper

2 tablespoons capers

8 ounces Gorgonzola cheese

1/2 fresh lemon

Dissolve the yeast in the warm water for 15 minutes. Add 1 tablespoon olive oil to the yeast water and stir.

Put 2 1/4 cups flour and 1 teaspoon salt in the bowl of a food processor. With the machine running, pour the water-yeast mixture through the feed tube and run until a dough ball forms. Add more flour if necessary to make a smooth, soft dough ball. Scoop out the dough into an oiled bowl, cover, and let rise for 2 hours.

Preheat the oven to 450 degrees F. and put in the pizza stone to heat if you have one. Otherwise wait, and use a large lightly oiled pizza pan or baking sheet. While the dough is rising you can prepare the toppings.

Push the dough down with your knuckles, then transfer it to a lightly floured work surface. With a floured rolling pin, roll out the dough, starting from the center and working out to the edges all the way around. Turn over and repeat on the other side until it reaches the thickness and size you would like. No need to be perfect; the pizza looks rustic if randomly shaped. Place dough on the pizza pan, baking sheet, or parchment.

Place the 2 cups basil leaves, garlic, Parmesan, 1/2 teaspoon salt, and 6 tablespoons olive oil into a food processor and process until well combined. With a basting brush, paint the basil-oil mixture (pistou) over the pizza, leaving 1/2 inch around the edges free.

Arrange the tuna, shrimp, red and yellow bell peppers, and capers over the pizza. Slice small pieces of the Gorgonzola over the top. Squeeze fresh lemon juice over everything. Drizzle with olive oil and bake for 15 to 20 minutes, until golden. (If you are using a baking stone, slide the pizza off the parchment paper onto the stone and bake.)

Slice the reserved 6 basil leaves thinly, sprinkle over the pizza, and serve.

Note: If you like a thicker crust, allow the pizza to stand with its toppings for 20 minutes before baking.

vegetables

Les Légumes

BROCCOLI POLENTA WITH TOMATO SAUCE
La Polenta de Brocoli à la Sauce Tomate

Vive le Veggie! Niçoise cooks are passionate about vegetables, which make their entrances to the table in rustic casseroles, stuffed into sardines, baked with cheese or polenta, or turned into a ratatouille. Cooked and raw vegetables served on a communal olive wood platter, with a small bowl of anchovy-flavored mayonnaise for dipping, is one of the delights of a mid-summer meal.

Anyone with a backyard has a multicolored vegetable garden with a good supply of Swiss chard, the vegetable of preference in the region, which finds its way into absolutely everything, from omelettes to desserts. Violet-tipped baby artichokes, brilliant orange and yellow zucchini flowers, baby spinach, fennel, gleaming eggplant, potatoes, vibrant green and red peppers, onions, and tender carrots are also found in most gardens as well as in the many open-air markets.

This recipe for broccoli and polenta makes a full meal and is excellent with a simple salad.

Serves 4

FOR THE BROCCOLI POLENTA

6 cups water

2 cups coarse yellow cornmeal, corn grits, or polenta

1 cup raw broccoli florets, finely chopped

2 teaspoons salt

2 tablespoons coarsely chopped fresh thyme leaves

  freshly ground black pepper

FOR THE TOMATO SAUCE

2 tablespoons extra virgin olive oil, plus more for drizzling

1 medium onion, finely chopped

2 cloves garlic, finely chopped

$2\frac{1}{2}$ pounds tomatoes, coarsely chopped

$1\frac{1}{2}$ tablespoons sugar

1 teaspoon salt

$\frac{1}{4}$ teaspoon freshly ground black pepper

1 cup freshly grated Parmesan cheese

Oil a 10 x 14-inch baking dish, line it with plastic wrap, and oil the plastic wrap.

Bring the water to a boil in a deep saucepan and whisk in the cornmeal in a steady stream to prevent clumping. Turn heat down to low and cook for 15 minutes, whisking frequently to aerate and turn the mixture over. It will pop and splatter, so be careful. Don't worry if it also sticks to the bottom; this is normal and it will soak off later.

Switch to a wooden spoon, still over very low heat, and cook and stir frequently for another 10 minutes, until the mixture is very thick. Add the broccoli, thyme, 2 teaspoons salt, and pepper to taste. Cook for another 5 minutes, until very dry and stiff and the polenta is pulling away from the sides of the pan.

Scoop it into the lined baking dish, spreading evenly with a wet or oiled spatula. Wet your hands, and pat the mixture down with your palms to smooth out the top. Allow to cool; within 10 minutes it will be ready to cut. Lift with the plastic wrap, place the polenta on a cutting board, and slice into squares to yield the maximum amount of pieces. If you use a 3-inch glass or cookie cutter, it will yield 8 round pieces.

Heat the oven to 350 degrees F.

Meanwhile, to make the sauce, heat olive oil in a saucepan over medium heat and cook the onions until tender. Add the garlic and cook for another 2 minutes. Add the tomatoes, sugar, salt, and pepper, and bring to a boil; then turn down to a simmer and cook for 8 minutes.

Over a bowl or saucepan, drain the tomato sauce through a sieve, pushing the solids down with a spoon until you have a smooth tomato sauce beneath. Or you can put it through a food mill.

Ladle some of the tomato sauce onto the bottom of a baking dish large enough to hold the polenta slices in one layer. Lay the polenta pieces on top. Ladle tomato sauce over them. Drizzle with olive oil, sprinkle with Parmesan cheese, and bake for 25 minutes.

Niçoise Zucchini Tian
Le Tian de Courgette à la Niçoise

Originally painted a deep, warm orange, my house had weathered to a gentle shade of coral by the time I moved there. The wooden shutters were the silver-green of an olive leaf. The two together were typical of the harmony of colors in this corner of France. When I walked down from the village, I saw the colors of the house in relief against olive trees and the grey-green sheer cliffs of the gorge.

Just above the house were *restanques*—narrow terraces of land cut like steps up the slope of the hill—which are traditionally used to grow crops. The two above our house, filled with fruit trees, offered a stunning view of the towering cliffs, the waterfalls in the canyon of the Gorges du Loup, and the village of Gourdon above. They also provided an excellent venue for entertaining on hot summer nights.

Since I was still looking for a dining room table, I often asked people over for picnics that I would serve outside on the restanques. We'd take a couple of big tablecloths and spread them under the trees and light some votive candles. Everyone would line up in the kitchen to be handed a platter or basket to carry up the hill.

That first summer, I learned how to make this tian, one of the many variations of vegetable tians you find in Niçoise cooking.

Serves 4

- 2 cups chicken broth
- 1 cup rice
- 4 medium zucchini
- 3 tablespoons extra virgin olive oil
- 1 onion, finely chopped
- 2 cloves garlic, minced
- 3 large eggs, beaten
- 8 basil leaves, finely chopped
- 1/2 teaspoon sea salt
- freshly ground black pepper
- cayenne pepper
- 1 1/2 cups grated Emmental or Gruyère cheese, divided

Heat the oven to 350 degrees. Oil a 6-cup gratin baking dish.

Bring the chicken broth and rice to a boil; reduce to a simmer and cook for 10 minutes. Drain and move the rice to a bowl.

Grate the zucchini on a box or flat grater, then squeeze dry with paper towels to eliminate excess liquid. Add the zucchini to the bowl.

Heat the olive oil in a skillet and cook the onions and garlic until lightly browned. Add them to the bowl.

Add the eggs, basil, salt, black pepper, and cayenne to taste, and 1 cup cheese; mix well to combine. Pour into the gratin dish, sprinkle remaining 1/2 cup cheese over the top, and cook for 40 to 45 minutes, or until golden on top.

ABOUT TIANS

A *tian* is an earthenware baking dish and is one of the items most commonly found in Niçoise kitchens. Recipes that are made in the dish are referred to as *tians*. Most often in Nice, tians are made either of colorful layers of vegetables or to resemble a crustless quiche, like the recipe facing.

LITTLE STUFFED VEGETABLES
Les Petits Farcis

Miniature stuffed vegetables are sold everywhere in the narrow streets of old town in Nice, as well as in super-markets, *traiteurs*, and open-air markets. If small enough, mini vegetables are served as amuse-bouche in elegant restaurants along the Côte d'Azur. The Niçoise love snacks, and these little bites are one of the most popular. I like to serve them either before dinner as a prelude and tease, just one or two per person, or as a vegetable side dish, four to six per person.

The quantity of stuffing it takes for the vegetables will depend on their size. So if you have bigger vegetables, this recipe will not fill them all; whereas, if you have small vegetables, this recipe should provide ample stuffing. This is a starting point to begin with; tailor as you go. Making the vegetables all the same size increases visual appeal. Any leftover vegetables can be drizzled with olive oil, sprinkled with fresh breadcrumbs, and baked along with the stuffed ones.

Serves 4

continued >

2   small white onions, peeled

2   Asian or other small eggplants, ends removed

2   small round or long zucchinis, ends removed

2   small round tomatoes

    salt, divided

2   small bell peppers, green or red

4   canned whole artichoke hearts

1   tablespoon fresh lemon juice

3   tablespoons extra virgin olive oil,
    plus more to drizzle

1   large onion, peeled and chopped

4   cloves garlic, minced

1/2 pound ground beef

1/2 pound pork sausage

1   cup cooked rice

3   tablespoons minced flat leaf parsley

1   tablespoon thyme leaves

3   eggs, beaten

8   green olives, pitted, minced

1/2 cup freshly grated Parmesan cheese

1/2 cup fresh breadcrumbs

    freshly ground black pepper

1   cup freshly grated Parmesan
    or Emmental cheese

Select a casserole dish big enough to hold all of the stuffed vegetables so that they can stand upright while baking. Oil the dish generously.

Slice the onions in half. Bring water to a boil in a large saucepan and drop in the onions. Reduce to a simmer and cook for 4 minutes. Remove the onions with a slotted spoon, reserving the water, and drain. Scoop out the centers to leave 1/2-inch walls. Chop the centers and add to a large bowl.

Bring the pot of water back to a boil. Drop the eggplants into the water to cook for 10 minutes. Remove the eggplants, reserving the water, and drain.

Slice zucchinis in half vertically, and drop into the water. Lower to a simmer and cook for 4 minutes. Remove with a slotted spoon and drain; discard the water from the pot. Scoop out the centers of the zucchinis and the eggplants with a spoon, leaving 1/2-inch walls; chop the centers and add to the bowl. At this point you can slice the zucchinis and eggplants into 3-inch pieces to achieve smaller bites if you wish, or leave as is. If the zucchinis are small and round, or patty pan size, slice off the tops, scoop out the centers.

Slice the tomatoes in half; scoop out the seeds and pulp, leaving the walls intact, and add pulp to the bowl. Sprinkle the tomato halves with salt and turn upside down on a paper towel for 10 minutes.

If the peppers are small, slice off the stem ends. If they are bigger, slice the peppers in half vertically. Scoop out the insides and discard.

Pat the artichoke hearts dry and coat with the lemon juice.

Heat the oven to 350 degrees F.

In a skillet, heat the olive oil and sauté the onions and garlic for 2 minutes. Add the ground beef and pork sausage and cook until no longer pink. Add meat mixture to the bowl of vegetables. Add the rice, parsley, thyme, eggs, olives, 1/2 cup Parmesan cheese, breadcrumbs, 2 teaspoons salt, and pepper to taste to the bowl; mix well. This is the stuffing.

Stuff all of the vegetables and arrange them so that they are upright in the baking dish. Sprinkle with Parmesan or Emmental cheese, then drizzle olive oil over the tops of the vegetables. Bake for 30 to 35 minutes.

CHICKPEA, EGGPLANT AND ZUCCHINI FRITTERS
Les Beignets de Pois Chiches aux Aubergines et aux Courgettes

"Finish off the dish with lemon juice and season with salt and pepper."

I was reading the last sentence to this recipe, which had been mailed to me by the woman who sold kitchen appliances at the restaurant supply store where I bought my restaurant-size stove. Her speech had been sprinkled with one or two ancient *nissart* words, the kind found on signs in old Nice, so I turned to her as a possible culinary guide to the world of authentic Niçoise cuisine.

I am crazy about this recipe. It is a delicious treat, with a crispy outside and creamy inside, while boasting the healthy benefits of using protein-rich chickpea flour. I never asked her why the lemon juice, as these turn out beautifully without it, but I include the thought as something you can try if you would like. I sometimes serve the fritters three deep, stacked against a piece of fish, with a small side salad on the same plate for a casual summer meal, or alone with salad for a vegetarian dinner.

Serves 4

1 cup chickpea (garbanzo bean) flour

1/2 teaspoon salt, plus more

freshly ground black pepper

dash of cayenne pepper

1 teaspoon turmeric

1 clove garlic, minced

3/4 cups water

1 tablespoon extra virgin olive oil, plus more for frying

1 medium eggplant

1 medium zucchini

lemon juice, optional

freshly grated black pepper, optional

Whisk together the flour, salt, pepper to taste, cayenne, turmeric, garlic, water, and 1 tablespoon oil in a large bowl. It should be the consistency of heavy cream. Let the batter rest for 1 hour.

Meanwhile, slice the eggplant thinly, lay it in a colander, salt liberally, and let rest for 1 hour. Then rinse, pat very dry, and finely chop.

Heat the oven to 200 degrees F. Line a baking sheet with parchment paper.

Coarsely grate the zucchini. With paper towels, squeeze out any excess moisture.

Heat enough olive oil in a large skillet to fry the fritters, about 1/2 inch deep.

Mix the eggplant and zucchini into the batter. When the oil is shimmering hot, drop in batter by the level tablespoonful and flatten with a fork. Fry until golden brown, turn over, and fry the other side until golden brown; transfer to paper towels. When drained, move the fritters to the baking sheet to keep warm in the oven until ready to serve. Sprinkle with a little salt and optional lemon juice and pepper.

Swiss Chard with Pears, Raisins, and Candied Garlic
Les Blettes aux Poires, aux Raisins Secs et aux Pignons a l'Ail Confit

My recipe box was filling up with recipes from neighbors, the village priest, waiters, people I met in stores while we stood on line for the cashier, star chefs from cutting-edge restaurants, Pamela, Madame, Dave, the wife of the ex-chief of police, and countless other friends; a sommelier who worked in a wine store in Nice; people who worked behind the stands at open-air markets; and ones I found and tweaked from local newspapers.

The recipe cards were handwritten, dated, noted with the origin of the recipe, and given a star rating. Tasting notes and people I served them to were scribbled in the margins, as well as the names of guests who really liked the dish. Unbeknownst to them, they became my recipe testers.

The recipe card for this vegetable side dish, with a sweet kick from the raisins and pears, became worn and bent from use.

Origin of the recipe: Hennie, an elegant Dutch lady brought up in Nice who invited us to dinner every once in a while.

Star Rating: how many are there in the universe?

Serves 4

12 medium-size whole cloves garlic, peeled

5 tablespoons extra virgin olive oil, divided

1/2 cup dry red wine

1 1/2 tablespoons sugar

1/2 teaspoon sea salt

1/4 cup baking raisins

12 large stalks Swiss chard (red is nice)

1 Bosc pear

1/4 cup pine nuts

Bring a small saucepan of salted water to a boil, reduce to a simmer, add the garlic cloves, and cook for 5 minutes. Drain in a colander. Wipe out the same saucepan, add 2 tablespoons olive oil, and when it is shimmering hot add the garlic cloves and cook for 2 minutes, moving them about to lightly brown.

Off the heat, pour in the red wine carefully to prevent splattering, then put the pan on the heat again and simmer for 6 minutes. Add the sugar and salt, and cook over medium heat for 12 minutes more, or until the liquid has reduced to a syrup. Add the raisins, stir, remove from the heat, and reserve.

Clean and pat dry the Swiss chard. Remove the leaves from the stalks, roll them tightly, slice thinly, and then slice again horizontally. Slice off the rough ends of the stalks, then slice the stalks very thinly.

Peel the pear, slice thinly, and then dice.

In a large skillet, heat the remaining 3 tablespoons olive oil. Add the sliced stalks and cook on medium heat for 4 minutes. Add the leaves, pear, pine nuts, garlic and raisin mixture with syrup, and stir, cooking for a further 2 to 3 minutes. Taste for seasonings and serve.

BRAISED FENNEL
Le Fenouil Braisé

The vegetables have a shorter journey to the table than you do to get to the restaurant. That's a major reason why vegetable dishes taste so alive in this area. They might come from the small plot of earth behind the restaurant, from that morning's market in town, or from the restaurant owner's private garden at home.

Vegetables definitely take up a good part of the conversation when talking with anyone about Niçoise food. In other places I have lived, when asking what to bring to dinner or a party, the chances are I would be asked to bring wine or a dessert. Here, it was vegetables. "Why don't you make your beautiful braised fennel and bring it along to the party?" (More like boozy fennel, I would think. It's made with almost a bottle of wine!)

So, when asked to bring a vegetable dish, this is the one I normally prepare: my boozy, beautiful braised fennel.

Serves 4

2 large fennel bulbs

1 organic lemon

¼ cup extra virgin olive oil

4 cups dry rosé wine (about 1 bottle), divided

2 heads of garlic, cloves removed and peeled

   fleur de sel

Peel the tough outer stalks of the fennel bulbs with a vegetable peeler to trim off any blemishes. Slice off the stems, save the fronds, and slice the bulbs in half lengthwise.

Peel the rind from the lemon with a vegetable peeler. Slice off the white inside pith from the rind, and slice the rind into short, thin matchsticks.

In a large heavy pan, heat the olive oil over medium-high heat, then place the fennel bulbs in the pan flat side down—and don't be tempted to move them. Sear for about 7 minutes, until golden brown. Take a peek, and when they are ready, turn over and sear the other side until golden brown.

Pour in 2 cups of the wine, sprinkle the garlic cloves and lemon rind around the fennel, cover the pan, and simmer over low heat for 30 minutes.

Uncover, turn the fennel bulbs over to the other side, pour in remaining 2 cups of wine, and sprinkle with fleur de sel to taste. Cover and braise over very low heat for another 30 minutes, until the fennel is very soft and tender.

On my quest to learn more about cuisine Niçoise, I came across the name of Hélène Barale, legendary for being one of the best-known personalities for keeping the tradition of cuisine Niçoise alive. If you could get a seat inside her restaurant, you'd be handed a paper with the lyrics for "Nissa La Bella" so at the end of your meal you could join her sing-along about the glories of beautiful Nice. When you were ready for dinner, Niçoise dishes would begin to appear, transporting you on a culinary journey through the recipes she grew up with and loved.

Nissa la Bella

Ô ma belle Nice
Reine des fleurs
Tes vielles toitures
Je les chanterai toujours.
Je chanterai les montagnes
Ton si riche décor
Tes vertes campagnes
Ton grand soleil d'or

BAKED STUFFED ZUCCHINI FLOWERS WITH TOMATO SAUCE

Les Fleurs de Courgettes Farcies Cuites au Four, Sauce Tomate

In spring, there would be violets in the grass below the Madonna in the stone wall in my garden. They only grew right there, at her feet. The Madonna had the most amazing blue eyes and some mornings was covered with jewels of dew.

Offerings appeared, yet I never saw who left them. I suspected Madame, who would stop to visit her on the way to my kitchen door—clenching her hand and tapping it to her chest twice, then etching the sign of the cross with a thumbnail to her forehead. Someone before me had built an arch in the wall to protect the Madonna, but I never learned whom.

Rather than leave the offerings, I gathered them after what seemed like a respectable amount of time, and brought them inside. Mostly, the anonymous gifts were a small vase with a single flower. But in the summer, the single flowers gave way to glorious bundles of golden zucchini blossoms. How could I leave their transitory, fragile beings to wilt in the hot sun? If I ended up bringing them inside and cooking with them, I would always say a small prayer of thanks as I prepared them to my Madonna of the Violets for sharing them with my table.

Serves 4

1/4 cup extra virgin olive oil, plus
   2 tablespoons, divided

1 small yellow onion, finely diced

4 medium cloves garlic, minced, divided

1 (28-ounce) can Italian plum San
   Marzano crushed tomatoes

1 teaspoon sugar

1 teaspoon sea salt, divided

1/4 cup dry red wine

1/2 cup sweet onion (e.g.,
   Vidalia), finely chopped

1 medium zucchini, coarsely
   grated and squeezed dry

   freshly ground black pepper

1 tablespoon finely chopped fresh basil,
   plus 8 chopped leaves for garnish

1 cup freshly grated Parmesan
   cheese, divided

1 large egg, beaten

8 large zucchini flowers, rinsed,
   patted dry, inside pistils removed

3 tablespoons water

1/2 cup freshly grated Emmental cheese

To make the tomato sauce, heat 1/4 cup oil in a saucepan. Add the diced onion and cook on medium heat for 6 minutes. Add 2 cloves miced garlic and cook for 3 minutes, stirring frequently. Pour the tomatoes into a food processor, add the contents of the saucepan plus the sugar, 1/2 teaspoon salt, and wine; process until smooth. Return to the saucepan, bring to a simmer, and cook for 25 minutes.

Meanwhile, to make the stuffing, in a large skillet, heat 1 tablespoon olive oil, add the 1/2 cup chopped onion, and cook for 3 minutes. Add remaining 2 cloves minced garlic and zucchini, and cook for another 5 minutes on medium-low heat. Off the heat, add 1/2 teaspoon salt, pepper to taste, and 1 tablespoon chopped basil. Stir well to mix, then add 1/2 cup Parmesan cheese and egg, and mix well.

Preheat the oven to 400 degrees F. Lightly oil a baking dish big enough to hold the stuffed flowers.

Gently open the flowers and stuff with 2 tablespoons or more of the filling, twisting the tops of the flowers closed before laying them side by side in the baking dish. Add the water around them and bake the stuffed flowers for 10 minutes. Spoon a little of the tomato sauce over each stuffed flower, then top with a sprinkling of Emmental cheese and bake for another 5 minutes, or until the cheese has melted.

To serve, spoon a little of the tomato sauce onto each plate, top with 2 flowers, shower with chopped basil, drizzle with a little olive oil, and serve with the remaining 1/2 cup Parmesan cheese on the side.

CHICKPEA CRÊPES STUFFED WITH NIÇOISE RATATOUILLE

Les Crêpes de Pois Chiches avec Ratatouille à la Niçoise

When I was living in Paris as a newlywed, the lady down the hall took it upon herself, luckily, to teach me how to cook a few French dishes. One was to wrap melon slices in prosciutto. Not really French, but it was easy and well received by my husband. The second was ratatouille. She took me to the supermarket and showed me how the ingredients needed to make it were sold together in a package in the vegetable aisle. We brought one home, and within what seemed like only minutes, we had a delicious ratatouille.

I also remember her fondly for pointing out to me the symbol of a horse head above the butcher shop around the corner. "Do you know that he sells horse meat? It is very delicious, but I just wanted you to know." I nearly fainted.

Years later, in Nice, I learned an entirely different way to make ratatouille. It was invented in Nice as a way to make an inexpensive meal from what was in the garden. This ratatouille is inspired by the original recipe from Jacques Médecin. He emphasized that what makes Niçoise ratatouille different from other versions made in France is in the way it is cooked in stages and then composed at the end. I follow his steps almost identically, changing very little.

Niçoise-style ratatouille takes longer to make, so this is a good dish for a weekend when you have more time.

Makes 8–10 stuffed crêpes

FOR THE RATATOUILLE

1/2 cup flour

1 teaspoon sea salt, plus more

freshly ground black pepper

1 pound eggplant

1 pound zucchini

8 tablespoons extra virgin olive oil, divided, plus more if needed

2 sprigs fresh thyme, leaves only

1 large onion, quartered

1 pound bell peppers, a mix of red, green, and yellow if possible

2 pounds tomatoes

7 cloves garlic, finely chopped

25 leaves fresh basil

1 tablespoon tomato paste

1/2 cup dry white wine

FOR THE CHICKPEA CRÊPES

4 cups chickpea flour

1 1/2 tablespoons turmeric

2 1/2 teaspoons salt

12 cracks of freshly ground black pepper

3 tablespoons extra virgin olive oil

3 3/4 cups water

To make ratatouille, mix the flour, salt, and pepper to taste with a fork. Slice the eggplants and zucchini into 1/2-inch-thick slices and toss in the seasoned flour.

In a large skillet, heat 4 tablespoons olive oil and cook the eggplant over medium heat until golden brown. (If the flour is turning dark brown, your heat is too high.) Transfer golden brown eggplant to a large saucepan in which you will be making the ratatouille.

Add more oil, if needed, and cook the zucchini until golden brown on both sides. Add to the saucepan and sprinkle a little salt, pepper, and one-fourth of the thyme leaves over the top.

Slice the onion wedges into 1/4-inch slices. Add more oil to the skillet if needed, and cook the onions for about 4 minutes, until they are almost golden. Add them to the saucepan.

Slice off stems from the peppers, seed them, and then slice thinly. Cook with a little oil in the skillet for 2 minutes, and then add to the saucepan.

Slice and chop the tomatoes finely, taking care to retain the seeds and juice.

Carefully wipe out the skillet with a paper towel and heat 4 tablespoons olive oil. Add the tomatoes, garlic, a fourth of the thyme leaves (reserve the rest for later), 10 leaves of sliced basil, and salt and pepper to taste; simmer until it resembles a sauce, about 7 minutes. Whisk in tomato paste to blend.

Transfer the tomato sauce to the large saucepan with the vegetables, add the wine, and mix well.

Simmer for about 12 minutes, then add the rest of the basil and thyme and cook for another 5 minutes, until the vegetables are soft and tender. Taste and adjust for seasonings. Continue cooking if it has too much liquid. You want the ratatouille to be dry enough to hold its shape inside the crêpes, yet still be moist.

Let sit at room temperature until you stuff the crêpes. The longer it sits, the more the flavors come together. At this point, you could even refrigerate it and use it the next day.

To make the crêpes, whisk together the chickpea flour, turmeric, salt, and pepper with a fork; then mix in the oil and water and let stand for 1 hour.

Oil a 9-inch crêpe pan or 10-inch nonstick skillet with olive oil and set it over medium-high heat. When the oil is sizzling hot, pour in 1/2 cup batter and then tip and swirl the pan to evenly coat it with the batter, letting excess drip out onto a plate. Turn down the heat to medium and cook the crêpe about 2 minutes, or until it is dry on the top. Then flip and cook the other side. Remove to a plate, cover with a piece of parchment paper, and make the next crêpe.

To serve, place a crêpe on each plate, spoon a good amount of ratatouille down the center, then fold over the crêpe. Each plate should have two stuffed crêpes.

VEGETABLES WITH ANCHOVY DIP
Les Légumes à l'Anchoïade

When my friend Anna came back for a visit, I decided to introduce her to Dave, the wild Australian superyacht captain who once drove out of our driveway with a swordfish head in the passenger seat. Was this the perfect match for demure, down-facing-dog Anna, the spiritual searcher surviving on a raw—and now vegetarian—diet?

So I invited Dave to dinner one night. It was a whirlwind. All I remember is a blur of shy glances, spears of endive dripping in *anchoïade* sauce being lifted to each other's lips, and my Anna jumping into the passenger seat with Dave as they drove out our driveway.

Warning: this dish may drive total strangers towards impulsive, and quite possibly passionate, behavior!

Anchoïade is a pungent dip served with fresh or cooked vegetables. What differentiates this anchoïade from others made in Provence is that in Nice they add egg yolks to make a mayonnaise and fold in chopped Niçoise olives or finely chopped capers. Serve with toasted sliced baguette, chilled dry rosé wine, and a warning.

Serves 4

FOR THE DIP

3 large cloves garlic

3 anchovies in olive oil, drained

1 tablespoon lemon juice

2 egg yolks

1 cup extra virgin olive oil

1 tablespoon capers

FOR THE VEGETABLES

4 small red potatoes, or 16 fingerling potatoes

4 small or new carrots

2 hard-boiled eggs, halved

2 red bell peppers, stem and seeds removed, sliced into strips

1 small cauliflower, cut into florets

1 zucchini, sliced into long strips

1 small fennel bulb, sliced thinly

4 small tomatoes, quartered

4 radishes, halved

2 endives, sliced in half lengthwise

1 bunch of fresh parsley

Drop the garlic into a mini food processor or blender while it is running to mince. Add anchovies and lemon juice and process.

With an electric mixer, beat the egg yolks in a small bowl until thick and pale. Beat in the garlic and anchovy mixture.

Slowly drizzle in the olive oil while continuously beating to make a thick mayonnaise; then fold in the capers by hand and scoop the dip into a serving bowl.

Boil potatoes in water to cover for 8 to 10 minutes, or until just tender. Drain and cool to room temperature. Boil carrots in water to cover for 4 minutes, or until just tender. Drain and cool.

Arrange the cooked vegetables, eggs, and raw vegetables on a platter with a bowl of the anchoïade dip in the center for dipping, and serve.

Offer sprigs of fresh parsley in a small vase on the table for a refreshing last bite after the meal.

Deep-Fried Vegetables with Sage
Les Légumes Frits à la Sauge

A paper plate. A rough-hewn wooden picnic table. A glass of apricot-colored wine. My shoulders and back are warm from the noonday sun, and my table companions are a couple who had come in on a cruise ship and stopped for lunch on their walk around town.

In old town Nice, we are enjoying just-fried tender zucchini flowers and a plate of deep-fried miniature vegetables, the kind that would be the polite size to serve Alice at tea time. I'm in a culinary wonderland of fried food.

Forget what they say about fried food. Here, the Niçoise are expert at keeping the oil hot enough so there is no trace of it in your food, and at keeping the quantities they give you down to three or four pieces. I would venture to say that if all food was fried to the level of perfection achieved in these old back streets and the portions kept to the size they serve, the merits of fried vegetables would be re-examined.

In the fall when the olives are ready to be harvested, I invite friends over to help. This thank-you of just-fried vegetables, like the ones found in old Nice, is waiting for them when they return from the field. They also get a share of the crop to take down to the Opio olive mill in exchange for a bottle of oil.

Serves 4

1 1/2 cups all-purpose flour

1/2 cup cornstarch

1 teaspoon baking powder

1/2 teaspoon sea salt

freshly ground black pepper

dash of cayenne pepper

1 teaspoon fresh sage, minced

1 3/4–2 cups white wine (or sparkling water, beer, or flat water), divided

Vegetable oil for frying

1 head broccoli, broken into florets

2 medium zucchini, sliced into 1/2-inch pieces

3 red bell peppers, sliced into rings

2 small eggplants, peeled and sliced into 1/2-inch pieces

2 small onions, sliced into rings

large caper berries with stems on, optional

fleur de sel

Vigorously whisk the flour, cornstarch, baking powder, salt, black pepper to taste, cayenne pepper, sage, and 1 3/4 cups wine together until the batter is the consistency of heavy cream. If it is too thick, add more wine or water, 1 tablespoon at a time, to thin it out. I usually use just shy of 2 cups liquid.

Heat the oil in a deep pan or skillet to 360 degrees.

Cooking in batches, dip the vegetables into the batter, remove with tongs, and carefully lower into the hot oil to fry until all sides are golden brown. Remove with a slotted spoon, drain on a wire wrack or paper towels, shower with fleur de sel and pepper to taste, and serve.

ROASTED WINTER VEGETABLES
WITH POLENTA PARMESAN CROUTONS
Les Légumes d'Hiver Cuits au Four,
Les Croûtons de Polenta et Parmigiano Reggiano

We were surprised to learn when we purchased our house that it had no heat. Many of the houses in the area were second homes, used for summer vacations, and ours had been one of them. And although the climate of the Côte d'Azur is subtropical, during winter months it can suddenly turn cold from winds driven down from the snow-capped mountains behind us.

Our first winter, we tried out the idea of relying on our enormous fireplace to heat the house. Icy winds swept through the hallways. The dogs even jumped onto the bed to curl up next to our warm bodies.

It was on a night like this that my husband innocently poked his head around the corner to ask, "How about that vegetable thing you make with croutons? And maybe some . . . "

I remember, uncharacteristically, of course, snapping back, "Great idea! After I roast and bake, I'll leave the oven door open to heat the house!"

We got heat the next year, two odd-looking heaters that were mounted above one hallway door and another door nearer the bathroom. My husband could still be relied upon to poke his head around the kitchen door asking for this dish, although with heat, I was a bit less snappy. It's a warming dish, perfect for a cold winter night, with or without heat.

Serves 4

FOR THE CROUTONS

3 cups water

1 cup quick-cooking polenta

1 tablespoon fresh thyme leaves

1/2 teaspoon sea salt

freshly ground black pepper

dash of cayenne pepper

1/4 cup freshly grated Parmesan cheese

FOR THE VEGETABLES

6 tablespoons extra virgin olive oil,
plus enough for frying croutons

1 tablespoon minced fresh rosemary

1 teaspoon minced fresh sage leaves

1/2 teaspoon sea salt

freshly ground black pepper

1 small butternut squash or pumpkin,
peeled, seeded, cut into 1-inch cubes

4 medium carrots, sliced lengthwise,
then into 1-inch slices

8 Brussels sprouts, halved

4 parsnips, cut into 1-inch slices

4 fingerling potatoes, halved lengthwise

1 beet, peeled, cut into 1-inch cubes

1 whole head garlic, separated
into cloves, peeled

Line an 8 x 5-inch baking pan or casserole with plastic wrap extending over the sides to use as handles to lift the polenta out of the pan. Oil the plastic wrap.

To make the polenta croutons, bring the water to a boil, then shower the polenta into the water while whisking in a circular motion, to prevent clumping. Whisk for 1 minute, then switch to a wooden spoon and scrape the bottom frequently, as towards the end of the cooking time it will become thick. At that time, stir in the thyme, salt, black pepper to taste, cayenne pepper, and Parmesan. Stir vigorously and continue cooking until it begins pulling away from the sides of the saucepan.

Pour cooked polenta into the lined baking dish, spreading it out evenly. Wet your fingers and gently pat the top to smooth it. Cover with plastic wrap and refrigerate for 30 minutes. Remove the polenta from the baking pan, set it on a cutting board, and slice into 1/2- to 1-inch squares.

Preheat oven to 425 degrees F.

In a large bowl, whisk together the 6 tablespoons oil, rosemary, sage, salt, and pepper to taste. Toss all the vegetables in the oil, then arrange on a large, shallow baking pan and bake for 25 to 35 minutes, or until the vegetables are fork tender.

Meanwhile, heat 1/4 inch of olive oil in a large skillet. When it reaches 350 degrees on a thermometer, begin frying the croutons until golden brown on both sides. Transfer them to paper towels to drain, and sprinkle with a little salt.

Spoon the vegetables into a serving bowl or individual plates, drizzle with a few drops of extra virgin olive oil, and top with the golden croutons.

easy weeknights

Les Dîners en Semaine

Tuna in Rosé Wine over Tagliatelle
Tagliatelle avec une Sauce de Thon, Tomate, Olive Noire et Rosé de Bellet

Dozens of varieties of organic tomatoes grow in the same area of Nice as the grapes that produce my favorite local wine, Bellet. I had gathered both on my shopping trip, so I thought, why not combine the two in a sauce, maybe even throw in some tiny Niçoise olives. A terroir marriage that now only needed, perhaps, fresh tuna. Yes! And some pasta to bring it together. That's how this dish evolved.

Use the best ingredients available to you: vine-ripened tomatoes or sugar-sweet cherry tomatoes. Use fresh herbs snipped at the last minute. Serve it with a glass of good chilled rosé, of course.

Serves 4

16 ounces dried tagliatelle or fettuccini

7 tablespoons extra virgin olive oil, divided

1 large onion, minced

4 cloves garlic, minced

3 cups dry rosé wine

8 fresh tomatoes, coarsely chopped

1 teaspoon minced fresh rosemary

20 oil-cured black olives, pitted and sliced

2 pounds fresh tuna steak, sliced into 16 slices

sea salt

freshly ground black pepper

6 fresh basil leaves

14 cherry tomatoes, halved

Cook the pasta according to package instructions. Toss it in 2 tablespoons olive oil, and keep warm until ready to use.

Heat 5 tablespoons olive oil in a skillet over medium heat; add the onion and cook for 3 minutes. Add garlic and cook for 2 minutes.

Add the wine, tomatoes, rosemary and olives; simmer for about 8 minutes, or longer if you would like to reduce the sauce more.

Baste a hot grill pan or large skillet with olive oil and place over high heat. Rub the pieces of tuna with olive oil and place on the grill pan or skillet. Sear both sides and cook to the degree of doneness you prefer. I like mine very rare. Remove from the heat and sprinkle with salt and pepper to taste.

Ladle enough sauce over the pasta to coat when tossed, reserving the remaining sauce to drizzle over the top or serve on the side. Arrange fresh tuna on top. Snip fresh basil leaves all over the tuna, and top with cherry tomatoes.

BELLET WINE

Award-winning Bellet wines are extremely rare outside of Nice, because fewer than 100,000 bottles are produced each year and the Niçoise love to buy their local wines. Most of the bottles are snapped up, even though they are relatively expensive. Bellet will only grow rarer as the small vineyard owners become tempted by developers to sell their prized land, with its panoramic views to the sea and the Alpes.

Bellet wines are produced by a dozen vineyards located in the hills behind Nice. The Bellet wine appellation, which includes whites, rosés, and reds, is one of the smallest wine appellations in France. The vines are thought to have been introduced to the area by the ancient Phoenicians around 2000 BC and are some of the oldest vines in the country.

The white wines are made from the Rolle grape, also known as Vermentino in Italy, which produces a fragrant, full-bodied wine. The red wines are made from Braquet grapes, native to the area, as well as with Folle Noire grapes. The white grapes allowed in a Bellet rosé wine are Blanqueiron, Bourboulenc, Roussanne, and Clairette; and the red grapes allowed in a Bellet rosé are the Braquet or Folle Noire.

One of the best descriptions of Bellet wines is found in Colman Andrews' book, *Flavors of the Riviera*, pages 278–83, in which he highlights the foods and wines found along the 125-mile stretch between the Italian Riviera and Nice.

The Bellet wines I like to have on hand are from these two vineyards:

Chateau de Cremat
442 Chemin de Cremat
06200 Nice
Telephone: (33) 04 92 15 12 15
Visits: Monday to Friday, 9 am – 5 pm. Book tasting
visits in advance.

Clos St. Vincent
Collet des Fourniers
St. Roman de Bellet
06200 Nice
Telephone: (33) 04 92 15 12 69
www.clos-st-vincent.fr
Visits: by appointment Monday to Saturday for
tasting and cellar visit.

HONEY AND VERMOUTH-ROASTED PORK TENDERLOIN WITH FIG VINAIGRETTE SALAD

Le Filet de Porc Rôti au Vermouth et au Miel, sa Salade à la Vinaigrette de Figue

The way I started giving cooking classes came out of the blue, literally. A stewardess on the Delta Airlines flight that flew direct between New York City and Nice had fallen for a man who lived in Cagnes-sur-Mer, who was as much a gourmet cook as she was too busy to be one.

When I gave dinner parties on weekends, I'd tell everyone to bring whoever was staying with them, because when you live in a sunny, beautiful place, everyone seems to have a constant stream of visitors. So Lucy the stewardess was brought along one weekend, and as she left, she asked if I would give her a cooking class so she could make a special meal for her new love interest. Surprised but delighted, I signed on *tout suite*, making a date for her to come back to my kitchen on her next flight. Then I thought and thought about what to teach her to cook. I wanted to give her something that was quick to prepare, as she said she would have very little time to make it, yet something interesting.

This is the dish I taught Lucy and ended up adding to future cooking classes I offered after word spread within the surrounding community of Americans and Brits. I gave her a basket of figs from my trees that were dropping dozens daily in my driveway, a pork tenderloin, a bottle of vermouth, and a bottle of honey before she drove out of my driveway. She mastered the recipe with ease and told me, with flushed cheeks and sparkling eyes, that she was on her way down to his house to make it for dinner that night.

Lucy became one of my first repeat cooking students, signing up with me on long layovers and staying over on nights when Mr. Right was not so right. I called her "Lucy in the Sky with Diamonds."

Serves 4

FOR THE PORK

1 cup honey

1 cup sweet or dry vermouth

$^1/_2$ teaspoon sea salt

    coarsely grated black pepper

1 tablespoon fresh lemon juice

1 whole pork tenderloin, 1$^1/_2$ pounds

FOR THE SALAD WITH FIG VINAIGRETTE

$^1/_4$ cup extra virgin olive oil

1 teaspoon Dijon mustard

2 tablespoons sherry vinegar
    or red wine vinegar

1 teaspoon honey

$^1/_2$ teaspoon salt

    freshly ground black pepper

1 cup fresh figs, sliced

4 handfuls arugula

In a bowl, whisk the honey, vermouth, salt, lots of pepper, and lemon juice to combine. Baste the pork loin with the honey mixture and let sit for 15 minutes while the oven is heating.

Preheat oven to 450 degrees F.

Place a roasting rack in a roasting pan, put the pork on the rack, and pour all of the honey mixture over the top. Cook pork in the oven for 20 minutes, until a meat thermometer reads 145 to 150 degrees F.

Allow the roast to rest 5 minutes before slicing and serving.

To make the vinaigrette, add the oil, mustard, vinegar, honey, salt, pepper to taste, and figs to a food processor and process until well combined. Taste and adjust seasonings.

Toss the arugula with just enough of the vinaigrette to coat, then divide among four plates. Arrange slices of pork over the salads, drizzling any remaining pan juices or vinaigrette over the top or around the plate.

VEGETABLES AND HARD-BOILED EGGS WITH HOT ANCHOVY AND GARLIC DIP
La Bagna Cauda

It is natural that *bagna cauda*, which comes from the Piedmont region in northwest Italy, would find its way into the food culture of Nice. Both had been part of the Kingdom of Sardinia from 1720 to the late 1800s, until Nice was ceded to France in return for helping the Kingdom of Sardinia to annex all the other Italian states into one—with the Kingdom of Sardinia at its head.

Nice's connection to Italy lives on in its centuries of love for bagna cauda, a hot dip made from olive oil, anchovies, and garlic.

I get my bagna cauda fix at one of my favorite restaurants in Nice, Le Safari. I often settle into a comfortable banquette in the back room dining area after shopping in the open-air market and order just the bagna cauda, as it is such a huge dish for one. They serve a basket filled to overflowing with fresh vegetables: baby violet artichokes, celery, fennel, a wedge of red cabbage, quartered endive, cauliflower florets, carrots, scallions, large mushroom caps, a couple of radishes, quartered radicchio, red and green peppers, a hard-boiled egg in the shell, and a handful of mesclun salad at the bottom of the basket. The hot dip for the vegetables is served to the side in a fondue pot set over a warming flame.

The chilled vegetables are exquisite against the heat of the dip. I grab for the celery first and drag its leaves through the dip, then work my way down the stalk. I break the shell of the egg and slice the egg into the dip, mashing it with a fork. It adds a layer of richness and calms the intensity of the anchovies. The flavor of anise on the tongue from fennel, the richness of the egg and anchovy, the freshness and crunch of the celery, and the sweetness of the red pepper, all create a heady symphony of flavors and colors.

I make it at home with whatever vegetables are ready in my garden. I also like serving it with slices of baguette to sop up any wayward dip. This is a wonderful dish for sharing at a table. Amplify it by preparing two pots of dip, and place a large serving platter in the middle of the table with a fabulous display of all the vegetables. A basket of sliced baguette, a nicely chilled white wine, and you have an easy and fresh summer dinner for two, or an appetizer for a few.

You will need a fondue pot with a flame underneath.

Serves 4

fresh raw vegetables, chilled

4 hard-boiled eggs in the shell

FOR THE DIP

4 cups best-quality extra virgin olive oil

7 large cloves garlic, finely minced

pinch of cayenne pepper

1 tablespoon fresh white breadcrumbs

10 anchovies, chopped (salt packed are
ideal, or substitute canned in olive oil)

1 tablespoon fresh lemon juice

1 crusty baguette, sliced

Prepare whatever vegetables you have on hand by washing, drying, and arranging them—as well as the hard-boiled eggs—attractively in a bowl or basket.

In a saucepan, heat the olive oil, then add the garlic, cayenne, and breadcrumbs; cook for about 3 minutes.

Add the anchovies and cook for 8 minutes, whisking to break the anchovies down and blend well into a smooth sauce. Add the lemon juice and whisk until incorporated and thoroughly heated. Taste and adjust seasoning.

Pour the hot dip into a fondue pot set over a flame and serve beside the vegetables and a bowl of baguette slices.

Note: bagna cauda, in a smaller quantity, is also excellent drizzled over grilled fish or shrimp as a sauce. Add some lemon zest or fresh orange juice for a delicious variation.

Le Safari Restaurant
1 Cours Saleya
06300 Nice
Telephone: (33) 04 93 80 18 44
www.restaurantsafari.fr

GRILLED SWORDFISH OVER RICE IN VIERGE SAUCE
L'Espadon Grillé avec du Riz, Sauce Vierge

I had scored some beautiful swordfish at the market in Cannes one day and came home excited to do something with it. So I called our fish expert, wild Dave the superyacht captain, and asked him for the recipe for the swordfish he had cooked for us one weekend.

"Do you have a pen? I'm just about to cast off but I can give you some ideas. Here goes."

Wild Dave was not so wild and wooly when it came to cooking. As he dictated very precise instructions to me, I could hear him in the background shouting out orders to his crew to begin casting off, and could hear his boss, the owner of the superyacht, purr beside him. Dave told us the owner was a beautiful Lebanese woman who wore fabulous jewels, could swear with the best of them, and liked to sit beside him when they left and returned to harbors to check out everyone else's yachts. We thought he had a terribly glamorous life.

"And the great thing about swordfish is you are eating all the fish of the sea when you eat them, because they dine on bluefish, squid, barracuda, tuna . . ." His enthusiastic tutoring gradually faded away as they made their way out to sea. I got enough of what he said to make the meal he wanted to teach me. This was what I wrote down.

I remember thinking, as I made it that night, how amazing our life was turning out. We had arrived in our village knowing no one and now had an ever-widening circle of friends, in all walks of life and all ages, tied together because of our common love for food and cooking, and for sharing with each other the way of cooking we had assimilated throughout our lives. I thought, with knowledge people become the same, their differences quickly falling away. From wild Dave from Australia to the women in my village, we easily linked together as if one. It was making me very happy.

Serves 4

2 cups long-grain rice

4 cups water

sea salt

FOR THE VIERGE SAUCE

1/2 cup extra virgin olive oil, plus more
to drizzle in rice and on swordfish

1 teaspoon Dijon mustard

3 medium tomatoes, finely chopped,
with the juice and seeds

1 lemon, juiced and zested

2 cloves garlic, minced

1 tablespoon capers, chopped

1 small shallot, minced

2 tablespoons fresh basil, minced

1 tablespoons flat parsley leaves, minced

1/2 teaspoon sea salt

freshly ground black pepper

16 large green pitted olives,
coarsely chopped

8 cherry tomatoes, yellow,
orange or red, quartered

salt

freshly ground black pepper

4 (6-ounce) swordfish fillets

2 lemons, wedged

In a large saucepan, add the rice, water, and 1 teaspoon salt and bring to a boil. Turn down the heat, cover the pot, and cook on a low simmer for 15 to 20 minutes, until done. Turn off the heat, drizzle a little olive oil over the rice, and toss to barely coat. Cover the pot.

Meanwhile, make the vierge sauce. Put 1/2 cup olive oil in a large bowl with the mustard and whisk until cloudy. Add the tomatoes, 2 tablespoons of lemon juice, lemon zest, garlic, capers, shallot, basil, parsley, salt, pepper to taste, olives, and cherry tomatoes; mix well with a fork. Taste for seasoning. Pour in extra olive oil if you would like a thinner sauce. Cover to allow the flavors to get to know each other until ready to use.

Heat the grill to medium-high. Rub the swordfish steaks with olive oil and season with salt and pepper. Place on the hot grill and cook for about 2 minutes; then turn and cook the other side for 2 to 3 minutes. The cooking time depends on how thick the steaks are, so test to see if they are done to your liking.

Pour three-fourths of the vierge sauce into the rice and toss with a fork to thoroughly coat; add the rest if you wish and toss well again, or save it to drizzle on top of the fish. Taste and adjust seasonings. Divide the rice among four plates and top with a grilled swordfish steak. Serve with wedges of lemon.

ONE-PAN CHICKEN DINNER
Une Casserole de Poulet et Légumes

Pamela gave me a lesson on how to use a napkin after she made this dish.

I must have made a faux pas, picking up a wing with my fingers, and wiping them on my napkin, because after dinner she discretely took me aside to show me how it's done. "Fold your napkin in thirds lengthwise on your lap. That way, when you open up the top fold, you can use the inside to wipe your mouth and fingers, then cover it up again with the top fold so your dinner companions don't see a messy napkin."

For our purposes, I encourage you to eat your roast chicken with fingers if you wish and with gay abandon. Just remember to fold your napkin in thirds on your lap!

Serves 4

1   (5-pound) chicken

    extra virgin olive oil

2   teaspoons sea salt, plus more

4   potatoes, quartered

4   onions, quartered

8   medium carrots, whole

2   lemons, sliced then halved

4   sprigs rosemary, leaves only, chopped

4   whole bulbs of garlic

Heat the oven to 400 degrees F. Brush olive oil over the bottom of a large roasting pan.

Place the chicken in the middle of the pan, breast side up. Generously salt and pepper the cavity, oil the skin, and then sprinkle it with salt. Bake for 30 minutes.

Remove the roasting pan from the oven and add the potatoes, onions, carrots, lemons, and rosemary.

Slice the tops off the garlic bulbs, rub with olive oil, sprinkle with salt, and add to the roasting pan.

Drizzle the vegetables with olive oil, sprinkle with salt, and return the baking dish to the oven for another 30 minutes. Test the chicken with an instant-read thermometer. If it hasn't reached 165 degrees F., continue cooking until it does, testing again after 15 minutes. The total cooking time should be between 1 and $1^{1}/_{2}$ hours.

Remove the roasting pan, leave the vegetables intact, and allow everything to rest for 10 minutes.

I like to bring the roasting pan to the table or a side table and let people serve themselves. Toss the vegetables in the pan so they are coated with the lemony rosemary oil at the bottom. Give each person a whole bulb of roasted garlic.

Note: Roast two or three chickens at once and you'll have an easy dinner party for a crowd!

MUSSELS IN CREAMY PERNOD SAUCE
Les Moules à la Crème de Pernod

Many years ago, when I was living in Paris, a friend invited us to the country for the weekend, and one afternoon we found ourselves sitting across from the legendary cookbook author Simca Beck. Our host had prepped us in advance that we would be visiting one of the most famous French cooks and cookbook authors in the country.

I remember being seated at a simple wooden table outside in the garden. She emerged from the house with a tray carrying tall glasses, a carafe of water, and a bottle of Pernod. She graciously poured the Pernod into each glass, added a splash of water, and nodded towards us with a smile to take one. My husband and I began to delicately sip our drinks while our host and Simca dove into an animated discussion.

My eyes burned and my heart beat faster. This was strong! And I didn't know if I really liked the taste. No, I decided I didn't. So when Simca rose to go back into her house for some olives and nuts to go with our drinks, I asked our host, "What do I do? Is it rude not to drink it all down?"

Without speaking, our friend smiled and put a finger to her lips. She held her own glass down at her side, aimed towards the grass, and simply poured some of it out, leaving a polite yet significantly smaller amount in the bottom of her glass. We discretely followed her lead before Simca returned.

It was not until years later that I finally tried Pernod again. And this time I loved it. It tastes a bit like licorice, and it has a myriad of uses besides making a summer drink. I learned to water it down considerably and to add ice. And I learned how to cook with it.

This is one of my favorite dishes using Pernod. I am sure Simca would approve.

Serves 4

- 5 pounds fresh mussels
- 5 tablespoons extra virgin olive oil
- 4 shallots, minced
- 6 cloves garlic, minced

- 2 small red or yellow potatoes, grated (about 2 cups)
- 2 1/2 teaspoons sea salt, divided
- 2 cups dry white wine
- 3 tablespoons Pernod

- 2 egg yolks
- 2 tablespoons water
- 2 tablespoons fresh tarragon leaves, chopped
- 1 large baguette, sliced

Scrub and pull off the beards from the mussels, then plunge them into a bowl of water and allow to sit for 15 minutes.

Heat the olive oil in a large soup pot and cook the shallots, garlic, and grated potato with 2 teaspoons salt for about 3 minutes. Add the wine and bring to a boil.

Drain the mussels and add them to the pot; cover and bring back to a boil, then reduce the heat to a simmer and cook for about 4 to 5 minutes, until all the mussel shells have opened. If any haven't opened, discard. With a slotted spoon, transfer the mussels to a big serving bowl or four individual bowls.

Bring the remaining liquid back to a simmer, add the Pernod, and cook for 1 minute.

Whisk the egg yolks with the water and 1/2 teaspoon salt; then, off the heat, whisk the egg mixture into the sauce.

Return to medium heat, whisking continually until the sauce thickens without boiling. Taste for seasoning, then stir in the tarragon, which has a slight licorice flavor that goes well with the Pernod.

Pour the sauce over the mussels and serve with a baguette to sop up the broth.

ABOUT PERNOD

Since 1932, Pastis has been a popular aperitif in France. It derives its flavor from the distillation of star anise and contains licorice root, aromatic herbs, sugar and 40–45 percent alcohol. Because of the predominance of anise, it is considered in the same genre as ouzo and sambuca.

Paul Ricard created his recipe for pastis in 1932, while Pernod was founded in 1805. In 1975 the two brands of Ricard and Pernod merged, to now be called Pernod Ricard.

To serve as a drink, Pernod is diluted with water, which turns it opaque white.

Niçoise Stuffed Fresh Sardines
Les Sardines Fraîches Farcies à La Niçoise

One of the first cooking classes I gave was on how to prepare stuffed fresh sardines. I thought it would be fun to start teaching my students how to make the snacks we all loved so much when we shopped in Nice, and then move on to main courses that might take longer to prepare.

I had never worked with fresh sardines before I moved to the South of France, and from what I could judge from the looks they gave me, neither had my students.

"Ok, now cut off the head and tail with your scissors, then cut down the belly and remove the insides." Once we got over this hump and all had rushed to wash their hands, it was a breeze.

"Place your sardines on the cutting board in front of you, skin up, then press gently down all along the backbone. Turn the sardine over and lift off the backbone and throw it away."

Sighs of relief. And encouragement from me, "You've just butterflied sardines!"

I'm not sure they were initially as excited about it as I was, but by the time we'd whipped together the stuffing, filled them, cooked them, and eaten them, they were raving about the dish and asking for more wine.

Serves 4

12 fresh sardines

4 Swiss chard leaves

3 tablespoons extra virgin olive
   oil, plus more to drizzle

1 small onion, finely chopped

3 cloves garlic, minced

2 eggs, beaten

1 teaspoon salt

1/2 teaspoon white pepper

   dash of cayenne pepper

1 cup fresh breadcrumbs

1/4 cup all-purpose flour

2 lemons, wedged

If the sardines are not dressed, slice off the heads and tails with scissors, slit them along the underside and clean them under running water. Pat dry.

To debone, place sardines on a cutting board skin side up and with your finger tips press down firmly along the backbone. Turn them over and pull off the backbone.

Heat the oven to 400 degrees F.

Roll and slice the Swiss chard leaves, then chop finely.

In a skillet, heat the oil and cook the onions for 3 minutes; then add the garlic and cook for 3 minutes. Add the Swiss chard and cook until any liquid has evaporated. Remove the mixture to a plate and squeeze out any residual liquid with paper towels, then transfer to a large bowl.

To the bowl, add the eggs, salt, white pepper, cayenne pepper, breadcrumbs, and a drizzle more of olive oil or a little wine or water if you think it is too dry for a stuffing. This will depend whether you use homemade breadcrumbs or store-bought, so add liquid as needed to bring the stuffing together.

Oil a gratin dish or baking pan.

Slice the sardines in half lengthwise along where the backbone was. Dredge the skin side of the sardines in the flour. Arrange 12 sardine halves in the gratin dish, mound each with stuffing, then top with the other 12 sardine halves to make "sandwiches." Press down lightly on each to compact. Drizzle with olive oil and bake for 10 minutes, or until they are golden brown.

Serve with lemon wedges either immediately or later at room temperature. Serve 3 sardines per plate. A green salad will round out the meal.

Note: if you can't find fresh sardines, try trout fillets. Slice them into 2- to 3-inch pieces and prepare as above, or use fresh smelts. Raisins or pine nuts are sometimes added to the stuffing as well.

Lamb Sauté with Ratatouille Sauce and Potatoes
Un Sauté d'Agneau avec une Sauce de Ratatouille et Pommes De Terre

Le Colysé is a café in Opio, near where Julia Child lived in Plascassier. It's where you see husbands reading their paper over coffee while their wives do grocery shopping in the Carrefour Supermarket on the other side of the parking lot. There's always an interesting mix of Dutch and English who live nearby, mixed up with French interior designers and gardeners. It's the kind of place where everyone has seen each other at least once before, and therefore must walk around shaking everyone's hand before sitting down.

One of my favorite dishes that sometimes shows up as their *plat du jour* is a quick sauté of lamb in a simple ratatouille sauce. I asked the chef how he makes it, and this is a pretty close rendition.

Serves 4

8	whole small potatoes, unpeeled
2	pounds boneless lamb stew meat, cut into bite-size pieces
1 1/4	teaspoons sea salt, plus more for lamb
1/2	teaspoon freshly ground black pepper, plus more for lamb
4	tablespoons extra virgin olive oil, plus extra
1	cup onion, minced
1/2	cup minced green bell peppers
8	whole cloves garlic
2	cups dry white wine
4	medium tomatoes, skin on, coarsely chopped
16	cherry tomatoes, halved
4	tablespoons minced flat leaf parsley

In a pot of boiling water, cook the potatoes until tender. Cool, peel, and then carve into ovals with a small knife (this is the way they do it, a classical French presentation that looks nice on top of the sauté). Keep potatoes warm.

Sprinkle the lamb with a little salt and pepper.

In a large skillet, heat 4 tablespoons olive oil, and when it is shimmering hot add half the lamb and brown on all sides. Remove to a platter and add the rest of the lamb, browning it on all sides. Add to the platter.

Add to the skillet the onions, peppers, whole garlic cloves, 1 1/4 teaspoons salt, and 1/2 teaspoon pepper. Stir and cook for 10 minutes. Add the wine, scrape the bottom of the pan to lift any bits, and simmer for 4 minutes.

Add the chopped tomatoes, cherry tomatoes, and lamb, and simmer another 4 minutes.

To serve, ladle into four individual shallow bowls or plates, making sure that each plate has 2 cloves of garlic, and top with 2 potatoes. Drizzle a little olive oil over the potatoes, shower each dish with 1 tablespoon parsley, and serve.

As you eat this dish, you mash the potatoes and whole garlic cloves down into the sauce.

Le Colysé Brasserie
1 Carrefour de la Font Neuve
06650 Opio

JULIA CHILD LIVED IN PLASCASSIER, NEAR OPIO

"France was my spiritual homeland: it had become part of me, and I a part of it, and so it has remained ever since." —Julia Child

In 1963, Paul and Julia Child built a small stone house in Plascassier on the property of her cookbook collaborator, Simone "Simca" Beck. They named it La Pitchoune, the little one, and it is where Julia wrote much of *Mastering the Art of French Cooking*. They owned the house from 1963 through 1992.

Today, you can visit Julia's Kitchen and dine where she gave her last dinner party at her beloved Pitchoune if you sign up to take a cooking class at the culinary program held there. For more information, visit www.cookingwithfriends.com.

SHRIMP WITH LEMONY AÏOLI
Les Crevettes avec un Aïoli de Citron

Everyone had been telling me about a shellfish restaurant in Nice that had oysters so good that Italians would drive over the border just to eat there. On my first visit to Café de Turin, I remember sharing with my husband a platter of oysters that were the biggest I had ever seen, tasting both sweet and like salt water. We sat in the old part of the restaurant that has been there since 1908. Its walls were stained from cigarette smoke (smoking is no longer allowed) and its bar had a worn patina from the elbows of legions of seafood lovers.

Our two-hour lunch began with succulent oysters washed down with a crisp, chilled Muscadet wine. We moved on to a platter of smoked salmon served with squares of dark rye bread and lemon wedges, large chilled shrimp with mayonnaise, and finished with a chilled seafood salad. Giddy from our feast, we sauntered down the street to a pastry shop and sat down for espresso and little lemon tarts drizzled with bitter chocolate.

When I make shrimp the way it is served at Café de Turin, I add my own touches, spiking the mayonnaise with garlic and lemon juice to make a lemony aïoli. I chill the shrimp and arrange them in a beautiful bowl for the center of the table, serving with the aïoli and an ice bucket with chilled wine on the side. A simple and quick meal, it's as good on New Year's Eve as a starter as it is for a casual lunch on a hot summer day.

Serves 4

2 pounds medium to large shrimp, with shells

2 egg yolks, room temperature

1 teaspoon Dijon mustard

1/2 teaspoon sea salt

pinch of cayenne pepper

1 cup extra virgin olive oil

1/2 cup vegetable oil

1–2 tablespoons fresh lemon juice, divided

2 teaspoons lemon zest

2 large cloves garlic, minced or pressed

In a pot of boiling water, cook the shrimp just until they turn pink. Drain, cool, and refrigerate at least 1 hour.

With an electric beater and bowl, or in a stand mixer, beat the egg yolks, mustard, salt, and cayenne until thick and pale. Then, while beating, add the oils, drop by drop until half used; then add the oils in a thin stream while beating until you achieve a mayonnaise consistency.

Add 1 tablespoon lemon juice and the zest and blend well. Taste for seasoning, and add the remaining tablespoon of lemon juice if you would like the aïoli to be more lemony. Add the garlic and beat once more. Store in the refrigerator until ready to use.

Pile the shrimp in an attractive bowl, spoon the aïoli into another bowl, and set both in the center of the table. Be sure to provide ample napkins, as people will be peeling the shrimp then dipping into the aïoli. I know it sounds formal, but I also put out a bowl of water with lemon slices floating on the top for people to dip their fingers in before cleaning their hands with their napkins after what can be a fun but slightly messy shrimp feast.

NIÇOISE COD
La Morve à La Niçoise

Brilliant emerald green drops of basil oil drizzled over a warm tomato and wine sauce at serving releases a heady fragrance. This is the epitome of a summer dish you would find in restaurants along the Côte d'Azur, and it is one of the favorite recipes in my cooking classes. It's quick to make and beautiful to serve.

Normally this dish calls for salt cod, but in the interest of creating a quick meal, I use fresh cod.

Serves 4

1 cup extra virgin olive oil, plus 2 tablespoons and enough for frying

1/2 cup fresh basil leaves, finely packed

1/2 teaspoon salt

8 fingerling potatoes, sliced

1 small onion, finely chopped

4 cloves garlic, minced

3 medium tomatoes, seeded and chopped

2 tablespoons chopped pitted green olives

1 tablespoon capers, finely chopped

1 cup white wine

1/4 cup Cognac (optional but traditional)

4 (6- to 8-ounce) cod fillets

1 cup all-purpose flour seasoned with salt and freshly ground black pepper

4 tablespoons minced flat leaf parsley

To a blender, add 1 cup oil, basil, and salt and blend for about 1 minute. Place a sieve over a bowl and pour the basil oil into the sieve, pressing down with the back of a spoon to capture all the oil. Reserve the oil in the bowl.

Heat an inch of water in a skillet, add the sliced potatoes, and cook at a simmer until they are fork tender. Drain and reserve.

Heat 2 tablespoons oil in a large skillet, add the onion and garlic, and cook for 3 minutes. Add the potatoes, turn gently in the skillet to coat but not break up, and keep warm.

To another large skillet, add the tomatoes, olives, capers, and 2 tablespoons basil oil. Add the wine, bring to a simmer, and cook for 5 minutes. Add the Cognac, if using, and cook for another 5 minutes.

Heat oil for frying in a separate large skillet. Dry the cod with paper towels, dredge in flour, then add to the skillet and fry until golden on all sides.

Bring the tomatoes and wine back to a simmer.

Divide the potatoes among four plates, place the cod on top, then pour the wine and tomato sauce around each piece of cod. Drizzle a little of the remaining basil oil over the top of the cod, then sprinkle each with 1 tablespoon of minced parsley and serve.

EGG NOODLES WITH CHICKEN, ANCHOVIES, OLIVES AND MUSHROOMS

Les Nouilles aux Oeufs avec le Poulet aux Anchois, aux Olives et aux Champignons

With bold strokes, the man in the window was laying down bright swaths of color on a canvas. I stopped to watch him paint, then couldn't resist any longer and entered his shop. I was in the village of Tourettes-sur-Loup, where artists have ateliers where they work and sell to passersby.

By his wooden palette covered with blobs of paint was a chipped bowl holding his lunch. Although the smell of drying paint was evident, an aroma as spirited as the colors with which he painted crossed the air between us.

"My sister cooks lunch for me and brings it to me every day. Her cooking sells more paintings than I could on my own!" I have to say, it was an interesting proposition. I was drawn in to talk about his art and stayed to talk about food. He graciously shared with me her recipe as he could guess she made it, and offered to give me painting lessons after I told him how much his art moved me. I love random spontaneous bursts of big color, which his style glorified. We made a date for my first class and for my first lunch cooked by his sister. I asked if she would make this dish and was able to flesh out the recipe further than my original notes and now make it almost as well as she does. I still don't paint as well as he does, but I'm working on it.

Serves 4

4 tablespoons all-purpose flour

2 teaspoons salt, divided

freshly ground black pepper

8 chicken thighs, skin on

4 tablespoons extra virgin olive oil, divided

1 whole bulb garlic, about 10 cloves, finely chopped

1 large shallot, finely chopped

2 cups dry white wine

4 sprigs fresh thyme

5 anchovies in oil, drained, minced

1 cup green pitted olives, halved

1 cup chicken stock

10 ounces mushrooms, cleaned and thickly sliced

12 ounces wide egg noodles, cooked

Heat the oven to 350 degrees F.

Combine the flour, 1 teaspoon salt, and pepper to taste on a plate; then drag the chicken thighs through the flour to coat both sides. Shake off excess.

In a large skillet, heat 3 tablespoons olive oil until quite hot, then fry the chicken thighs on medium-high heat until golden brown, about 8 minutes. Don't let the chicken turn dark brown; if it starts to get too dark, turn down the heat. Transfer chicken pieces to a plate.

In the same skillet, add 1 tablespoon more olive oil and cook the garlic and shallot until tender, about 3 minutes. Add the wine and 1 teaspoon salt, then scrape the bottom of the pan with a spatula to release any cooked bits. Simmer the wine for about 3 minutes. Add the thyme, anchovies, and olives and mix well.

Put everything from the skillet into an ovenproof baking dish and arrange the chicken on top. Add the stock.

Cut a piece of parchment paper a bit smaller than the shape of the baking dish, and place gently over the top. This will allow a little moisture to escape, but not all of it, while the chicken is cooking. Cook the chicken in the oven for 35 minutes. Add in the mushrooms, return to the oven, and cook for another 10 minutes.

Meanwhile, cook the pasta and keep warm.

Remove chicken from the oven and discard the sprigs of thyme.

To serve, arrange pasta on four individual dishes, ladle the hot sauce over the pasta, toss, then place 2 pieces of chicken on top.

MOUNTAIN TROUT IN WINE SAUCE WITH MUSHROOMS
La Truite, Sauce Vin Blanc aux Champignons

There's a high-altitude world of mountain climbing, fishing, hunting, and bungee jumping hidden from the mainstream flow of life below on the Riviera, a hint of its existence emerging when you order mountain trout from a menu in town. Trout are fished in rivers sourced from snow melting and flowing down from the alpine peaks behind Nice to the sea.

Wild rivers—la Vésubie, la Tinée, le Boréon, and le Var—surge over boulders, stop to make deep pools, then continue down steep inclines, making great fly-fishing territory. The Loup—one of the best-known rivers, begins at over 4,000 feet above sea level and tumbles down over 50 miles to the sea. Trout thrive in the gin-clear icy water, and if they are caught they are brought to the market and snapped up by local restaurants.

If I see a couple in the fish market in Nice, I grab them and bring my prize home. This is one of the ways I cook them.

Serves 4

4   whole trout (have the fish monger clean, scale, and dress them)

    salt

    freshly ground black pepper

1   lemon—1/2 sliced, 1/2 juiced

4   tablespoons olive oil, divided, plus more to coat trout

3   cloves garlic, minced

2   tablespoons finely chopped flat leaf parsley

1   cup dry white wine

1   pound small button mushrooms, halved

Heat the oven to 375 degrees F.

Clean and pat dry the trout. Cut diagonal slashes on each side of the trout, season the cavity with salt and pepper, and place slices of lemon inside. Oil the outside of each trout with olive oil.

In a skillet, heat 2 tablespoons oil and cook the garlic and parsley with 1/2 teaspoon salt and pepper to taste for 2 minutes. Whisk in the wine and lemon juice. Taste for salt and adjust if needed.

Pour the sauce into a baking dish, then arrange the trout in a row over the sauce. Cover with aluminum foil and bake for 20 to 30 minutes, depending on the size of the trout. Cook until a thermometer reads 140 degrees F. when inserted into the middle of the fish, and the flesh easily flakes with a fork.

Meanwhile, heat 2 tablespoons oil in a skillet, and when hot add the mushrooms and cook on high until they are golden.

To serve, place one trout on each dish, spoon the sauce around it, and topple the golden mushrooms over each fish.

SWISS CHARD OMELETTE
La Trouchia

Somewhere between an Italian frittata and an omelette, *la trouchia* is made in many homes in the Niçoise countryside as a simple weeknight meal or to take on a picnic because it travels well.

Although you can sometimes find it cold and sliced into squares at bars around Nice, my favorite place to enjoy it is at a tiny restaurant just off the Cours Saleya, called On Est Pressé. They prepare it on the premises with lots of ground black pepper in the mix. Mine is a variation of theirs and includes the addition of garlic, shallots, and Parmesan cheese.

Serves 6

3 cups fresh Swiss chard leaves, tightly packed

5 tablespoons extra virgin olive oil, divided

2 medium shallots, minced

4 cloves garlic, minced

8 medium eggs, room temperature, beaten

6 ounces grated Parmesan cheese

6 fresh basil leaves, torn into small pieces

2 tablespoons pine nuts

1 teaspoon salt

freshly ground black pepper

2 medium tomatoes, seeded, finely chopped

Wash the Swiss chard leaves. Squeeze them in a paper towel until they are very dry, then roll, slice into thin pieces, and coarsely chop.

Heat 2 tablespoons oil in a skillet and cook the shallots and garlic for 3 minutes.

In a large bowl, place the eggs, Swiss chard, cheese, basil, pine nuts, salt, lots of pepper, and the onion-garlic mixture. Mix well with a fork.

Heat 2 tablespoons olive oil in a nonstick skillet until quite hot, then pour in the egg and chard mixture and cook over medium-low heat. With a spatula, press the chard leaves down, then cover the skillet and cook for about 12 to 15 minutes, or until the underside is golden brown. Check by lifting up the edges with a spatula.

Remove the lid, place a large plate over the skillet, and turn upside down. Add 1 tablespoon of olive oil to the skillet and slip the *trouchia* back into the skillet from the plate to cook the other side for 10 to 15 minutes. Slip the trouchia out onto a large serving plate, slice, and serve with a topping of the raw chopped tomatoes.

sunday suppers

Les Dîners de Dimanche

Caramelized Pork Roast with Olive Jam
Un Rôti de Porc Caramélisé avec ses Légumes et une Confiture d'Olive

"Madame Davis! Madame Davis!" I heard someone calling frantically.

I ran out my kitchen door to the patio and looked down the driveway. There was Monsieur, waving his arms and pointing past the village chateau to the mountains. "Madame Davis! The wild boars are coming! They are driving them down from the hills. I just closed your gates! Keep them shut and keep your dogs inside. They will be running down the road here soon!"

Wild boar. I felt a chill, remembering the look of their sturdy tusks when I first saw them in an autumn market. I checked on the dogs. Fine. Wild boar, I thought. Aren't they good to eat?

I tasted one that winter at the Auberge de Caussols, a rustic country restaurant in the village above Grasse. It was in a *daube de sanglier*, served in its own shiny little copper pot, sided with homemade raviolis. Although the dish was superb and I would order it again, at home I prefer to use the tame version to make a pork roast.

Serves 6

FOR THE MARINADE AND ROAST

2 oranges

3 tablespoons fennel seeds

1 tablespoon fresh rosemary

6 cloves garlic (4 whole cloves, plus 2 cloves minced)

1 shallot

4 tablespoons olive oil, plus more

2 cups dry white wine, divided, plus some to keep pan moist

8 tablespoons honey, divided

2 teaspoons sea salt, plus more

¼ cup dark brown sugar

3 pounds boneless pork loin roast

2 tablespoons granulated sugar

1 tablespoon sherry vinegar

FOR THE OLIVE JAM

1½ cups pitted canned black olives, drained

½ jar oil-cured black olives

½ cup sugar

olive oil to thin

FOR THE VEGETABLES

6 large sweet white onions

6 whole carrots

6 whole garlic bulbs

olive oil

sea salt

6 Yukon gold potatoes, quartered

Auberge de Caussols
4313 Route Departementale 12
06460 Caussols
Telephone: (33) 04 93 09 29 67
www.aubergedecaussols.com

Zest one orange and juice both. Put the juice and zest in a bowl big enough to hold the pork roast.

In a food processor, pulse the fennel seeds, rosemary, 4 cloves garlic, and shallot until finely minced. Add this mixture to the bowl. Add the olive oil, $1\,^1/_2$ cups wine, 4 tablespoons honey, salt, and brown sugar; whisk well.

Put the pork in the bowl, rub the marinade all over the outside, cover the bowl with plastic wrap, and refrigerate overnight. If you can fit the pork in a large ziplock bag with the marinade, this works as well.

Meanwhile, make the olive jam. Coarsely hand-chop the pitted canned black olives and add to a saucepan. Squeeze the pits out of the oil-cured olives to yield about $^1/_2$ cup olive pieces. Add to the saucepan along with the sugar, and bring to a boil on medium to high heat. Let it bubble away until the liquid is reduced, the sugar is dissolved, and it has a smooth consistency, about 4 to 5 minutes. Add a few drops of olive oil to thin out if desired, stir vigorously until smooth, cool, and reserve until ready to serve with the pork.

Remove the pork from the refrigerator, pat dry, and reserve the marinade.

Heat the oven to 350 degrees F.

Lightly oil a roasting pan. Place the pork roast in the center of the pan. Pour the marinade over the pork and into the roasting pan. Roast in the oven for 1 hour and 15 minutes. As the marinade evaporates, add a little more white wine to the roasting pan. After the roast has baked for 25 minutes, sprinkle 2 tablespoons granulated sugar over the top.

Oil a baking dish for the vegetables and fill it with the whole onions, carrots, whole garlic bulbs sliced in half, and potatoes. Drizzle with olive oil and sprinkle with salt. Place in the oven at the same time you sprinkle the roast with sugar.

When a meat thermometer shows the internal temperature of the pork has reached 160 degree F., remove the roast to a carving board or serving platter. Cover with a loose tent of aluminum foil, and allow to rest for 15 minutes before slicing. Remove the vegetables from the oven when the vegetables are fork tender.

To make a sauce, place roasting pan on the stove over low heat, add $^1/_2$ cup white wine, and scrape the bottom of the pan to lift up any browned bits. Turn heat up to medium, add remaining 4 tablespoons honey, sherry vinegar, 2 minced cloves garlic, and salt to taste. Whisk to blend.

Serve the pork roast with the sauce, roasted vegetables, and olive jam. Leftovers make tasty pork roast sandwiches spread with olive jam.

TOUR DE FRANCE ZUCCHINI PIE
Tourte de Courgettes Tour de France

Like dancers stretching at a ballet barre, the men from my village could be seen limbering their limbs over the stone ramparts during the Tour de France. One day they would be dressed normally, the next day suddenly appearing in skin-tight black bicycle shorts and close-fitting colorful tops broadcasting the name of their favorite team. Villages all across France have the same thing occurring when the Tour de France begins, as legions of bicycling fans sport their solidarity. So when our town heard that the Tour de France was to pass outside our village, people buzzed with anticipation.

A bicycling enthusiast, my husband joined the teams from neighboring towns every Sunday to pedal up and down dizzyingly steep hills for weekly exercise. The day the Tour de France was to visit our village, my husband disappeared with his *peloton* up the hill, while Madame walked down the hill with a picnic for us to take along.

We carried low canvas chairs and sat by the dusty side of the road for more than an hour, waiting for the great bicycle race to pass by. We heard clapping and shouts of encouragement down the road, so we knew they were approaching.

Whooooooooooooosh. Fifteen seconds and they were gone.

Our reward, we agreed, was more from the delectable pie she prepared than from the wind and whir of the bicycle wheels.

Madame's pie had a bottom and top crust, and the slices she brought stood at least a couple inches high with filling. Inside it was moist and savory, while the pie crust on the outside was tender and flaky. You can buy store-bought pie crust for this recipe, but taking the extra time to prepare a homemade one produces a far superior pie.

This would make a beautiful party dish or substantial family meal. Once you've tried and tasted it, you'll feel as if you won the Tour de France!

Serves 6-8

FOR THE FILLING

2 cups cooked rice

3 cups coarsely grated zucchini
(about 2 zucchinis)

3 tablespoons extra virgin olive oil

1 medium white onion, diced

3 cloves garlic, minced

$1^1/_2$ cups thinly sliced, tightly packed ham, diced

1 cup grated Emmental cheese

3 large eggs, plus 2 large egg yolks

$^1/_2$ teaspoon Dijon mustard

$^1/_2$ teaspoon honey

    freshly grated nutmeg

$^1/_2$ teaspoon salt

    freshly ground black pepper

FOR THE PIECRUSTS

$2^1/_2$ cups all-purpose flour

1 tablespoon sugar

$^1/_2$ teaspoon salt

$^1/_4$ teaspoon baking powder

2 sticks cold unsalted butter, cubed

4–5 tablespoons cold water,
plus more if needed

1 egg beaten with 1 tablespoon
water for an egg wash

Heat the oven to 375 degrees F. Have a 10-inch oiled springform pan ready to use.

To make the filling, begin by adding the cooked rice to a large mixing bowl.

Squeeze the grated zucchini in paper towels to eliminate any moisture, and add to the bowl with the rice.

Heat 3 tablespoons oil, add the onion and garlic, and cook on medium heat for 5 minutes. Add to the bowl. Add the ham and cheese to the bowl, and mix everything with a fork.

Whisk together the eggs, egg yolks, mustard, honey, nutmeg, $^1/_2$ teaspoon salt, and lots of freshly ground black pepper. Add to the bowl and mix well with a fork to combine.

To make the piecrusts, add the flour, sugar, salt, and baking powder to the bowl of a food processor; pulse 4 times. Add the cubed butter and pulse 15 times, until the mixture begins to look mealy; then pour in 4 tablespoons water and process. Pinch the dough to see if it comes together. If not, add 1 more tablespoon water and process.

Scoop out the dough onto a large piece of parchment paper and bring together with your hands into a ball. Slice the ball in half, wrap each half in plastic wrap, and refrigerate for 1 hour.

When you are ready to roll out the piecrusts, take one piece of dough from the refrigerator. Roll it out on a lightly floured work surface into a circle large enough to fit the bottom of the springform pan and reach at least halfway up the sides. Fit it into the pan. Pour in the filling and pat down with a spatula.

Roll out the second piece of dough to fit over the top of the pie with a little to spare. Lay it over the top of the filling and gently press down around the edges and against the walls of the pan to seal the two piecrusts together. Gently roll over the dough edges around the perimeter to create a stand-up crust, and then use your fingers to pinch into a ruffled shape. With a pastry brush, paint the top of the crust with the egg wash, and make 2 small knife slits in the center. Place the springform pan on a baking sheet, put into the oven, and bake for 35 to 45 minutes, until golden brown.

Remove from the oven and allow to rest for 10 minutes before releasing the spring, moving the pie to a serving plate, and slicing.

CHICKEN WITH BOILED VEGETABLES AND AÏOLI
Le Poulet Poché aux Légumes, aux Oeufs Durs et à l'Aïoli

Much of Provence celebrates special holidays and holy days with a Grande Aïoli, a feast to be shared that is comprised of poached salt cod, hard-boiled eggs, and cooked and raw vegetables. In homes and restaurants around Nice, however, an aïoli is also enjoyed any time of the year, in smaller scale, using anything from fish, meats, or chicken with vegetables. It's especially good in the summer with poached chicken, raw and cooked vegetables, hard-boiled eggs, sliced baguette, and a chilled rosé wine. Napkins required.

Serves 4

FOR THE AÏOLI

2   large egg yolks, room temperature

1/2   teaspoon water

1/2   teaspoon Dijon mustard

1/2   teaspoon salt

   dash of cayenne pepper

1   cup extra virgin olive oil

1/2   cup vegetable oil

   juice from 1/2 lemon

8   cloves garlic (less or more)

FOR THE CHICKEN AND VEGETABLES

1   (4-pound) chicken

1   carrot, grated

1   small onion, chopped

1   clove garlic, chopped

2   bay leaves

4   black peppercorns

8   small potatoes, boiled in their skins till tender

2   medium beets, peeled, cooked, halved

1   pound fresh green beans, trimmed and sliced in half

4   medium carrots, halved lengthwise, sliced into fourths

1   large fennel bulb, sliced into fourths

8   radicchio or endive leaves

4   medium tomatoes, quartered

4   hard-boiled eggs, halved

1   baguette, sliced

To make aïoli, place the egg yolks, water, mustard, salt, and cayenne in a bowl; with an electric hand mixer, beat until thick and pale. Drizzle in the oils drop by drop while beating, and when half used begin to pour in a thin, steady stream until the mayonnaise thickens. Whisk in the lemon juice; taste and add more salt if needed. Press the garlic into the mayonnaise and whisk to blend well. Chill until ready to use.

To poach the chicken, place it in a large pot with the carrot, onion, garlic, bay leaves, and peppercorns, and cover with water. Bring to a boil, reduce heat to a simmer, cover, and cook for 40 minutes, or until done. Transfer the chicken to a plate and allow to cool to room temperature.

To serve, carve the chicken and arrange the pieces and slices on a large serving platter. Surround it with raw vegetables on one side, cooked on the other, hard-boiled eggs and stacks of sliced baguette on either end. Serve with a bowl of aïoli for dipping and spreading.

GEORGES AUGUSTE ESCOFFIER

"Surtout, faites simple." ("Above all, keep it simple.")
—Georges Auguste Escoffier

My introduction to the perched village of Villeneuve-Loubet, a few miles away from Nice, resulted in the discovery that it was the birthplace of Escoffier—the fearless one, the one who stood French cuisine on its head by defining a different way of working in the kitchen that would forever redefine the cuisine. At twelve, he was working in his uncle's restaurant in Nice, a few years later worked his way to Paris, and from there nimbly climbed a steep ladder to the top.

There is a culinary museum in the village house where he was born. After doing much reading in the library there, I concluded that it was his simple background as the son of a blacksmith and as a son of the area and its culture that prepared him to approach the high temples of French haute cuisine with the straightforward approach he learned from his family and those cooking around him. I would go so far as to say it was his Niçoise upbringing that influenced his way of approaching cooking, allowing him to challenge and reinvent traditional French methods. He championed simplicity, efficiency, and food made with the freshest ingredients.

The Musée de L'Art Culinaire
Institut Joseph Donon
06270 Villeneuve-Loubet
Telephone: (33) 04 93 73 93 79
www.fondation-escoffier.org

DUCK WITH BIGARADE ORANGE SAUCE AND
DUCK FAT–ROASTED POTATOES
Le Canard Rôti , Sauce Bigarade, Pommes de Terre Rôties à la Graisse de Canard

This recipe, which calls for slow roasting a whole duck for more than 4 hours, produces a marvelous crispy skin. It is sided with a sweet-sour orange sauce that showcases the bitter bigarade oranges found growing in my village. *Bigarade*, a classic French sauce, was codified by the great chef Escoffier (see page 179), who grew up near Nice. If you can get *bigarade*, Seville, or bitter oranges, it works wonders with the rich taste of duck. If not, the vinegar in the sauce does the trick.

I've included luscious duck-fat roasted potatoes, as well as an optional garnish of toasts topped with slices of buttery fried duck liver. You have all the components for a complete meal in this recipe, but feel free to use all together or singly. Save the bones and what is left over after dinner and simmer in water to cover for a couple of hours for a flavorful stock you can use for soup or freeze.

Tip: Some ducks are more fatty than others, and fatty ones give off glorious duck fat that you can use in this recipe or save for another use. Muscovy ducks are lean. Pekin, Long Island, and Moulard ducks are fatty and best for rendering the most fat.

Duck fat is unsaturated and high in monounsaturated fats, as well as high in healthy linoleic acid. It fits well into the Niçoise style of cooking, ranking close to olive oil in health benefits, compared to those of beef or pork fat.

Serves 4

1 (5-pound) whole duck (free-range Pekin, or Long Island, if possible)

sea salt

1 small organic orange, cleaned and quartered, plus 3 medium organic oranges, zested and juiced

olive oil

freshly ground black pepper

2 cups water

2 pounds potatoes, scrubbed and quartered

8 whole cloves garlic, peeled, plus 2 teaspoons minced garlic

¼ cup sugar

3 tablespoons red wine vinegar

¼ cup dry white wine

½ cup bitter orange marmalade (Seville)

4 slices toast, halved diagonally, optional

Remove the duck from the refrigerator 1 hour before cooking. If it comes packaged with goodies inside the cavity, pull them out and reserve to make stock, and keep the liver separate to fry later and slice on toast. Wash and dry the duck, then pat dry.

Score the skin in several places over the top in a crisscross pattern, without slicing down to the meat, and prick 30 to 40 times all over the entire bird. The purpose of this is to allow fat to seep off during cooking, and the more fat that seeps from the skin, the crispier the duck will be. With tweezers, pull out and discard any sharp, pointy little quills. Trim any excess skin and put it in a saucepan over medium-high heat with 2 cups water, bring to a simmer, and cook until the fat has released from the skin, then strain the fat into a large measuring cup and reserve.

Put the innards (except the liver) and a sprinkling of salt in a saucepan with water to cover, and simmer until you have a flavorful stock.

Preheat oven to 300 degrees F.

Place the duck breast side up on a roasting rack in a roasting pan, tuck the wings under the duck, place 1 tablespoon salt and the quartered small orange inside the cavity, rub the entire duck with olive oil, and sprinkle with salt and pepper.

Roast in the oven for 1 hour. Remove from oven and use a turkey baster to siphon the duck fat from the bottom of the roasting pan into the large measuring cup, being careful to avoid hot spatters.

Turn the duck breast side down in the roasting pan, poke the skin in a few more places, and roast for 1 more hour.

Take out the duck as before, siphon off the fat and add it to the measuring cup, turn the duck over breast side up, return the roasting pan to the oven, and cook for 1 more hour.

Remove from the oven, siphon off the fat, and turn the duck breast side down. Toss the potato wedges and whole garlic cloves in duck fat from the measuring cup, sprinkle with salt and lots of pepper, and add them to the roasting pan. Cook for 1 more hour (for a total of 4 hours). When a meat thermometer shows the duck has reached 165 degrees F., it is done. You might want to baste the potatoes one more time with the duck fat you have accumulated in the measuring cup. Save any left over in the refrigerator.

Turn on the broiler and return the duck to the oven to crisp the skin for a few minutes, watching closely so that it does not char. You can leave in the potatoes if you think they need crisping as well. Remove from the oven, transfer to a carving board, and allow to rest at least 15 minutes before slicing. Keep the roasting pan juices.

While the duck roasts for 4 hours, you will have plenty of time to make the bigarade sauce and fried liver toasts.

To make the sauce, put the sugar and red wine vinegar in a medium saucepan over medium-low heat and cook until the sugar dissolves and starts to caramelize, becoming thick. Remove from the heat and pour in $1/2$ cup orange juice carefully, as it may splatter. Pour the stock you made from the duck innards into a measuring cup, and top up with water, if needed, to reach 1 cup; then add to the saucepan, whisking to blend well. Add the white wine.

While the duck and potatoes are resting, pour the bigarade sauce from the saucepan into the roasting pan juices, place the roasting pan over 2 burners on the stove, and deglaze the pan with the sauce, rubbing the bottom of the pan with a wooden spoon to release any bits. Bring to a boil and reduce the sauce by half. Taste for seasoning, adding drops of vinegar or orange juice to balance the sweetness, plus salt and pepper to taste.

Carve the duck as you would a chicken or turkey. Divide the meat among four plates, add the potatoes and whole garlic cloves on one side, drizzle the sauce over the duck (not on the crispy skin) and into a pool on the other side, and then top with fried duck liver toasts if desired. Serve with a simple green salad.

Optional: If you would like to make the fried liver toast garnish, quickly sauté the duck liver in olive oil with garlic, salt, and pepper, then slice into 4 pieces and put one on each toast, or mash with a fork and spread on the toasts. Balance a toast on top of the duck on each plate and serve.

PISTOU TOMATO TART IN A BASIL CRUST

La Tarte aux Tomates et au Pistou, Pâte de Basilic

We unfurled our blanket and sat down. Although it was early evening, the sand was still warm from the sun. The sea in front of us was choked with anchored yachts, while behind us, Canne's grand hotels were already twinkling with lights. It was the 14th of July, Bastille Day, and there would be a fabulous fireworks show over the water, choreographed to ballet music.

It became our annual tradition to take a picnic to the beach to watch the festivities. Every year we'd pack a large wicker basket with our dinner, china, and flutes for champagne. I would carry this tomato tart by hand, while inside the basket was usually a small cake. We would eat our meal and watch the exploding stars fall from the black sky to dissolve in the black sea. While many chose to sit at restaurant beach tables, we relished our front row seats on a blanket by the water's edge.

Serves 4-6

FOR THE CRUST AND TART

$1/4$ cup fresh basil leaves, plus 6
to slice into ribbons

1   large egg yolk, room temperature

1   stick unsalted butter, cold, sliced

$1/4$ teaspoon fresh lemon juice

$4 1/2$ tablespoons ice cold water, plus more
to bring dough together if needed

1   cup all-purpose flour

$1/2$ cup hazelnut flour, hazelnut
meal, or almond meal

$1/2$ teaspoon salt

1   teaspoon sugar

4   tablespoons pistou (recipe follows)

2   pounds tomatoes, different sizes
and colors, including cherry

10 pitted black or oil-cured black
olives, sliced, for garnish

FOR THE PISTOU

3   cloves of garlic, peeled

2   cups tightly packed fresh basil leaves

$1/4$ teaspoon sea salt

$1/2$ cup extra virgin olive oil

$1/2$ cup freshly grated Pecorino
Romano cheese

Oil a 10- to 11-inch round tart pan with a removable bottom, or a 10-inch springform pan.

Into the work bowl of a food processor that is running, drop the $1/4$ cup basil leaves and mince them. Add the egg yolk, butter, lemon juice, and water and pulse 8 times. Add the flour, hazelnut flour, salt, and sugar; pulse until just mixed and the dough looks like coarse meal. Do not process until it forms a ball. Scoop out the dough onto a piece of plastic wrap, gently bring it together with your hands, wrap it in the wrap, and press down with the heel of your hand to make a flat, round disc. Refrigerate the dough for 45 minutes or longer.

Roll out the dough on a lightly floured work surface between two pieces of parchment paper, and then place it into your tart or springform pan. I like to cut the dough a little bigger than the pan and fold it back over itself all the way around to make a crust that sits up a bit higher than the edge of the pan; this gives leeway for shrinkage when baking. Pinch it in a decorative way all the way around. Prick the bottom of the tart with a fork, then refrigerate another 25 minutes while you heat the oven to 400 degrees F.

Place a piece of parchment paper or foil in the pastry shell and weigh it down with uncooked rice or beans, and bake the shell for about 10 minutes. Remove the weights and paper, and bake for another 8 minutes, or until golden. Take out of the oven, leaving the oven on, and cool the crust to room temperature.

To make the pistou, pulse the garlic, basil, and salt in a food processor until it reaches a pasty consistency. With the machine running, slowly add the olive oil drop by drop, then in a thin steady stream until you achieve a thick paste. Scoop the paste out into a bowl and mix in the cheese with a fork until well blended.

Spread the bottom of the crust with pistou and shower the fresh basil ribbons over the top. Slice the tomatoes and arrange decoratively on top, then scatter the olives over the tomatoes.

Bake the tomato tart in the oven for 30 minutes, until cooked through. Allow to come to room temperature before slicing.

Pavé of Salmon with Summer Vegetables, White Wine Sabayon

Les Pavé de Saumon aux Légumes d'Été, Sauce Sabayon de Vin Blanc Salé

One day I had a meal at Keisuke Matsushima Restaurant in Nice that was composed of a savory mushroom sabayon topped with a ragout of wild mushrooms. Since then I have been encouraged by the chef's lead, preparing savory sabayons, loving their light-as-air texture.

This recipe is ideal made with summer vegetables and pairs well with a bitter salad of arugula or dandelion leaves barely coated in a simple vinaigrette.

Serves 6

- 6 medium carrots, halved vertically, cut into 2-inch pieces
- 12 fingerling potatoes
- 3 medium zucchini, halved vertically, cut into 2-inch pieces
- 1 (3-pound) center-cut salmon fillet, $1^{1}/_{2}$–2 inches thick
- extra virgin olive oil

- $^{1}/_{2}$ cup dry white wine
- chopped capers, small bowl
- fleur de sel
- freshly ground black pepper
- finely chopped tarragon and basil, optional

FOR THE SABAYON

- $^{1}/_{2}$ cup dry white wine
- 6 large egg yolks, room temperature
- sea salt
- 1–2 tablespoons fresh lemon juice, optional

Bring two pots of water to a boil then reduce to a simmer. Drop the carrots and potatoes into one pot, the zucchini into the other. Begin checking the vegetables after 5 minutes. When they are cooked until just tender, drain them in a colander and keep warm with aluminum foil placed loosely over the top.

Preheat oven to 350 degrees F. Select a baking pan large enough to hold the salmon; line it with foil and brush the foil with oil.

Rinse the salmon, pat dry, and lay it skin side down on the baking pan. Drizzle the top of the salmon with olive oil, pour the white wine around the fillet, and bake for 15 minutes, or until a meat thermometer reads 140 degrees F. Transfer the entire fillet to a large serving platter and cover loosely with aluminum foil until ready to serve.

While the salmon is baking, make the sabayon. Fill a saucepan half full with water and bring to a boil, then reduce to a simmer.

In a large heatproof bowl, put ½ cup white wine and egg yolks and beat with an electric hand mixer on high for about 4 minutes, or until the liquids have increased about four times in volume.

Place the bowl over the pot of simmering water, preventing its bottom from touching the water, and beat for about 4 to 5 minutes, until the mixture has firmed up and holds its shape. Do not allow the mixture to boil. Taste for seasoning, adding salt or lemon juice if desired. Remove from the heat and transfer to a serving bowl.

To serve, remove the foil from the salmon and arrange the vegetables around it. Pass the sabayon with a ladle for people to spoon it over their fish and vegetables. For garnishes, place a bowl of chopped capers nearby on the table, as well as fleur de sel and a pepper mill. If you would like to offer another garnish, a small bowl of finely chopped tarragon and basil is a wonderful addition.

ABOUT SABAYON

Sabayon is a technique of whisking egg yolks, liquid, and flavorings over a bain marie until light and foamy. Sabayon is either sweet or savory. The sweet version uses egg yolks, sugar, and sweet wine or spirits, while the savory versions use egg yolks, salt, and liquid—either water or dry white wine.

It is said that *zabaione*, which originated in the nearby Piedmont region of Italy, found its way to France when Catherine De Medici brought her chefs with her when she married King Henry II in the 1500s. Both cookbook authors that documented Niçoise cuisine, Mireille Johnston and Jacques Médecin, list Sabayon Niçoise as a sweet sauce that came from neighboring Piedmont. They explain that when it migrated to Nice, the traditional Marsala wine was dropped in favor of sherry, Port, Madeira, or a mix of rum and water.

With Nice's proximity to, and shared heritage with, Italy, it is not surprising this sauce shows up in various guises in Niçoise kitchens and restaurants. The version I encounter most frequently is savory, made with dry white wine and served with fish, scallops, or vegetables.

Niçoise Beef Stew
La Daube à la Niçoise

This is a basic French wine-soaked beef *daube*. Traditionally, daubes are cooked in a large earthenware or copper pot with a lid called a *daubière*, but any Dutch oven or heavy pot with a tight-fitting lid will do. In the traditional recipe cooked in Nice, there is often the addition of veal and pork in the form of shins and other cuts.

I encountered so many variations of beef daube over time that I began to feel comfortable adding my own touches to this recipe, including orange rind and olives, because I love the flavors that develop and it underlines its being from my village, the city of oranges.

Start marinating the meat the day before, then let it cook on the back of the stove for three or more hours, until it is tender. In Nice, they use leftovers from this stew to stuff ravioli and its sauce to spoon on top of the ravioli. It makes a fabulous filling and a thrifty second meal.

Serves 6

3 pounds boneless beef stew chuck, 2-inch cubes

4 cups dry red wine, or more to cover, divided

5 tablespoons extra virgin olive oil, divided

3 tablespoons dark brown sugar

6 cloves garlic (2 minced, 4 sliced), divided

6 strips organic orange rind, divided

4 tablespoons Cognac, divided

3 carrots, thickly sliced

1 large onion, coarsely chopped

2 large unpeeled tomatoes, chopped

2 tablespoons tomato paste

2 tablespoons orange marmalade

4 teaspoons fresh thyme leaves, divided

1 tablespoon all-purpose flour (not traditional)

1/4 cup water

1/2 cup pitted Niçoise, Gaeta, Kalamata or oil-cured olives, sliced

10 ounces mushrooms, thickly sliced

salt

freshly ground black pepper

egg noodles, cooked

Marinate the beef in a large ziplock bag overnight in the refrigerator with 1 cup wine, 2 tablespoons olive oil, sugar, the minced garlic, and 4 strips orange rind.

To make the daube, remove the meat the next day onto paper towels and pat very dry. Reserve the marinade.

In a large heavy pot, heat 3 tablespoons olive oil and brown the pieces of meat in batches over medium-high heat. After the meat is seared and browned on all sides, return it to the heavy pot.

Add the reserved marinade, 3 tablespoons Cognac, carrots, onion, tomatoes, sliced garlic, tomato paste, orange marmalade, 2 strips orange rind that you have chopped, 2 teaspoons thyme, and remaining 3 cups wine (or more) to cover the meat. Bring to a boil, then turn down to a simmer, partially covering the pot with a lid, and cook for at least 3 hours, until the meat is fork tender.

Mix flour into ¼ cup water until dissolved, then pour into the daube and stir well to incorporate.

Add 1 tablespoon Cognac, olives, and mushrooms, and simmer another 5 to 10 minutes, stirring occasionally to incorporate the flour as it slightly thickens the sauce. Add salt and freshly ground black pepper to taste. Serve over egg noodles and sprinkle with the remaining 2 teaspoons fresh thyme leaves.

These words from F. Scott Fitzgerald are engraved on a plaque hanging in the lobby of the hotel, his former home. The quote describes exactly the way I felt at that moment:

"With our being back in a nice villa on my beloved Riviera (between Cannes and Nice) I'm happier than I have been for years. It's one of those strange, precious and all too transitory moments when everything in one's life seems to be going well."
—F. Scott Fitzgerald, 1926, Juan-les-Pins

La Passagère Restaurant
Hôtel Belles Rives
33, boulevard Edouard Baudoin
06160 Juan-les-Pins
Telephone: (33) 04 93 61 02 79
www.bellesrives.com

PASCAL BARDET'S FISH FILLETS IN SAFFRON-SCENTED BROTH
Les Filets de Poisson dans un Bouillon Parfumé au Safran de Pascal Bardet

A Cole Porter song began to play in the recesses of my mind as I entered the lobby of Hôtel Belles Rives. It was almost as if a movie was being directed around me. A cast of characters emerged. A mood was set. The props, however, were real.

From stage left, a maître d'hôtel glided towards me, impossibly handsome and Fred Astaire debonair. I had been invited for lunch at the hotel's restaurant, La Passagère, and he showed me the way to my table outside on the terrace facing the sea. Then he told me the story of the hotel and I learned why I was feeling so enthralled with the setting and sense of place.

This was where F. Scott Fitzgerald worked on *Tender Is the Night*. He and his wife, Zelda, lived here for two years. Then it was called Villa St. Louis, and it is where they celebrated their *joie de vivre*, with enthusiastic visits from Hemingway after Fitzgerald's success with *The Great Gatsby*.

Chef Pascal Bardet now presides over the hotel's restaurant. Having worked seventeen years for Alain Ducasse at the Louis XV Restaurant in Monaco, he is the Chef de Cuisine of his own restaurant here at Hôtel Belles Rives. His cooking reflects modern cuisine Niçoise. "You can't talk about cuisine Niçoise without talking about the fishermen, farmers, and kitchen gardens that provide us all with the incredible produce to cook with. I have fishermen in little boats showing up at the dock of the hotel every day bringing me their prize catch. This is the essence of this style of cooking, using the best local ingredients possible," says Bardet.

On my way out after lunch, I passed through the Bar Fitzgerald. I drew my finger slowly along the keys of the black piano. I could smell Zelda's perfume as she passed by. She stopped at the bar, then turned back towards me with a playful smile, lifting her glass of champagne in my direction, *"Do you hear Cole Porter playing, his notes floating out on waves to the sea?"*

In Le Passagère restaurant, this dish is presented in a shallow bowl with the clear broth, potatoes, tomatoes, and olives around two fillets of St. Pierre fish (John Dory, in England) that are garnished with delicate green fennel fronds. I use tilapia or sea bass in the recipe; they work well. Call your fish market ahead of time to reserve fish trimmings (about 2 pounds) for the fish stock.

Serves 4

3 medium tomatoes

   sea salt

   freshly ground black pepper

3 tablespoons extra virgin olive
   oil, plus more for drizzling

3 cloves garlic (2 minced, 1
   chopped), divided

2 pounds mixed small fish or fish
   trimmings (heads and carcasses)

1 pound fish, cut in pieces (ocean perch,
   sea bass, or rock fish are preferable)

1 medium fennel bulb with stalks and fronds

1 onion, finely sliced

4 small cluster tomatoes, chopped

   a few threads of saffron or a
   little powdered saffron

   pinch of Piment d'Espelette
   or hot paprika powder

5 cups water

2 large 7-inch long potatoes, or
   3 large 5-inch potatoes

8 fillets tilapia, sea bass, or other firm-
   flesh white fish, skinless (ask the fish
   monger to prepare the fillets)

8 scallions

   fleur de sel

12 pitted Taggiasche olives (or Gaeta, Niçoise,
   or your favorite pitted black olives)

Preheat oven to 200 degrees F.

Peel, cut into quarters, and seed the tomatoes. Season with salt, pepper, a drizzle of olive oil, and 2 cloves minced garlic; then bake in the oven for $2\frac{1}{2}$ hours. Remove the roasted tomatoes until ready to use. (You can do this step a day or more ahead).

Put the fish trimmings and fish pieces in a large bowl of cold water, swirl with your hands, and drain into a colander. Discard the water.

Slice the stalks from the fennel bulb, and finely slice the bulb. With the bottom third of the stalks nearest the bulb, slice off 8 pieces, then slice them in half vertically. You will cook these later as a garnish. Chop the rest of the fennel stalks to add to the broth, and save the fronds.

To make the broth, heat 3 tablespoons olive oil in a large saucepan, and sweat the onion and sliced fennel bulb for about 3 minutes. Chop the fennel stalks and add to the pot, then add the chopped cluster tomatoes, 1 clove of chopped garlic, saffron, Piment d'Espelette or hot paprika, and the cut fish and fish trimmings. Cook on very low heat, stirring with a wooden spoon, for about 10 minutes. Then add 5 cups water and bring to a boil; turn down to a simmer and cook for 30 minutes. Drain through a chinois or fine sieve into a large saucepan and boil until the liquid is reduced to 4 cups. Take off the heat and reserve.

Slice the potatoes into 12 pieces that are $\frac{1}{3}$ inch thick by 1 inch in diameter. (The original recipe in French calls for the potatoes to be cooked *sous vide* at 90 degrees centigrade for 14 minutes). In a vegetable steaming basket set over boiling water, steam one layer of potato slices, covered, for anywhere from 5 to 8 minutes. When they are tender but not falling apart, remove and cool to room temperature. Continue to steam the slices of potato in the same manner until all are done. Steam the 8 pieces of fennel you saved in the vegetable basket over boiling water until just tender.

Slice the scallions vertically, then into small pieces. Drop them into the broth, bring to a boil, and cook until just tender. Remove the scallions, reserving the broth.

Steam the fish fillets in batches until all are done.

To plate, pour $\frac{1}{2}$ to 1 cup of the broth into each bowl, lay down 3 potato slices, layering the fennel and scallions on top. Arrange 2 fish fillets on top of the vegetables. Garnish with fennel fronds and a light sprinkle of fleur de sel. Divide the roasted tomatoes among the four dishes, placing them around the fish, and also place 3 olives along with them.

STUFFED SEA BASS
Le Loup Farci

While I kept fine china and crystal from my London days in the cupboard to pull out for special occasions, for everyday we ate from plates I fell in love with and bought at flea or antique markets in the area. We drank our wine from multicolored short water glasses hand-blown in Biot, the glass-blower's breath caught for all time in the air bubbles the glassware was famous for.

One of the treasures I came home with one day was a long, very heavy, white oval serving platter.

"What can you use it for?" my husband asked, frowning.

"Fish!"

I came up with that one rather quickly, but that's exactly what I bought to fit into my new serving dish.

It was a magnificent loup de mer, which was line-caught off the coast of Nice that morning; but any large sea bass can be substituted to make this simple, elegant dish. Your fish should smell fresh, the flesh should feel firm when you touch it, and the eyes should be clear. When you buy a whole sea bass, ask for it to be packed on ice in a plastic bag, if possible, to transport it home.

Serves 4

1   (2 to 3-pound) sea bass (or 4 [1$^{1}/_{2}$ pound] sea bass or loup de mer)

4   tablespoons extra virgin olive oil, divided, plus more for drizzling

2   shallots, minced

3   cloves garlic, minced

1$^{1}/_{2}$ cups fresh breadcrumbs

1   egg, beaten

$^{1}/_{2}$ jar capers, drained

8   oil-cured black olives, or green olives, pitted, finely chopped

1   teaspoon anchovy paste

4   tablespoons minced fresh parsley

1   orange, thinly sliced

1   zucchini, thinly sliced

1   potato, thinly sliced

    sea salt

4   lemons, sliced into wedges

Preheat the oven to 450 degrees F.

Wash the sea bass inside and out and pat dry.

In a skillet, pour 2 tablespoons olive oil, then add the shallots and garlic and cook 3 minutes. Remove from the heat and cool to room temperature.

To make the stuffing, put the breadcrumbs in a bowl, add the shallot and garlic mixture, egg, capers, olives, anchovy paste, parsley, and 2 tablespoons olive oil, and mix well.

Cut a piece of parchment paper big enough to hold the bass and place on a baking sheet or pan. Lightly oil the middle of the parchment paper and lay the bass down the center. Stuff the bass. Ring the bass with alternating slices of orange, zucchini, and potato. Drizzle the fish and vegetables with olive oil, sprinkle with salt, fold the parchment paper into a parcel so that no steam escapes, and bake for 20 minutes. Remove from the oven.

Transfer the entire parchment parcel to a serving platter, open, and serve with wedges of lemon.

WALNUT-CRUSTED CROUSTADES WITH WILD MUSHROOMS AND SCRAMBLED EGGS

Les Croustades aux Champignons Sauvages et à la Brouillade, Pâte de Noix

Dozens of cuckoo clocks hung side by side, crowded on the walls of the room. I was waiting with a friend in the study of a house for the man who was to take us foraging for mushrooms. Fascinated, we looked at each, wondering what it would look like when the cuckoos came out. Some of the clocks were little alpine chalets, some elaborate buildings.

"So you like my clocks?" he asked as he entered the room. His smile lit us up. "In a couple of minutes I can show them to you! I'll go get my gear and come right back."

A couple of minutes later, at noon, they all went off at once, totally delighting us.

My friend informed that me our guide, Klaus, was a well-known character, highly respected in the area as an expert forager of mushrooms and edible plants, which he harvested in the mornings before going to work in the high-tech industrial park in Sophia Antipolis. On his way to work, he would take the fruits of his morning foraging to a store in Tourettes-sur-Loup to sell. That's how I found out about him.

Klaus took us to the forest and helped us find apricot-colored girolles and beige-and-white ceps big enough for fairy folk to live in. He also showed us how to go to a pharmacist to make certain we hadn't picked anything poisonous. France, he said, has a huge network of pharmacists specially trained to pick over your wild mushrooms for you, because it is hard to distinguish the poisonous ones from the good ones. There are more than thirty fatal mushrooms lurking among more than two thousand varieties that are safe.

On my drive home that day, I stopped to pick wild thyme and rosemary, clinging to the now rain-drenched hills beside the roadway, and incorporated them into little wild mushroom tarts.

You can use just about any kind of mushroom in this recipe—except for canned. I make a free-form homemade walnut crust, but a good-quality prepared pie pastry also works. The recipe proceeds in stages, so read it through before beginning, as you will bring everything together at the end.

Makes one 11-inch tart or 4 individual tarts

1/4 cup walnuts

1 1/2 cups all-purpose flour

3/4 teaspoon sea salt, divided

1 teaspoon sugar

1 large egg, room temperature

1 teaspoon fresh lemon juice

1 stick unsalted butter, chilled
and cut into pieces

3 tablespoons very cold water,
plus more if needed

2 pounds mushrooms, cleaned and sliced

3 tablespoons extra virgin
olive oil, divided

1/4 teaspoon freshly ground black pepper

2 cloves garlic, minced

1 sprig rosemary, leaves only, minced

1 sprig thyme, leaves only

6 large eggs, beaten

1/2 cup freshly grated Pecorino
Romano or Fontina cheese

To make the crust, place the nuts, flour, 1/2 teaspoon salt, and sugar in the bowl of a food processor and process 6 seconds. Scoop out into a mixing bowl.

Add the egg, lemon juice, butter, and water to the food processor, pulse 6 times, then process for 7 seconds.

Add the flour mixture back into the processor and pulse just until the mixture comes together, stopping before it forms a ball. If the dough does not come together enough, drizzle in a tablespoon of water and pulse until it just begins to form a ball.

Scoop out onto a large piece of plastic wrap and gently bring the dough together with your hands. Wrap the dough with the wrap, then with the heel of your hand press down to make a flat disc. Refrigerate for 1 hour.

Toss all of the mushrooms with 2 tablespoons olive oil, 1/8 teaspoon salt, 1/4 teaspoon pepper, garlic, rosemary, and thyme.

Heat the oven to 400 degrees F. for 15 minutes. Line a baking sheet with parchment paper.

Remove the dough from the refrigerator and roll it out between 2 sheets of parchment paper to an approximately 1/8-inch-thick square or rectangle. Either make one large free-form tart or cut into small round tarts with a knife or round glass.

In the center of each shape, whether small or large, make a pile of the mushrooms and fold over the edges of the dough towards the center, pinching to keep the dough together to create free-form tarts, leaving a center opening large enough to see the mushrooms and spoon in scrambled eggs.

Bake tart(s)on a baking sheet lined with parchment paper in the oven for 20 minutes, until browned. After the first 10 minutes, begin to prepare the scrambled eggs.

Heat 1 tablespoon olive oil in a sauté pan and add the 6 beaten eggs with 1/8 teaspoon salt. Scramble the egg mixture. When you remove the tart(s) from the oven, spoon the eggs on top of the mushrooms, sprinkle with the grated cheese, and serve immediately.

BONE-IN RIB STEAKS WITH ROASTED MARROWBONES
Les Tranches de Bifteck avec des Os à Moelle

The French Riviera has been beloved territory to so many artists that it would take weeks to visit all the galleries and museums that hold their work.

"Can you see why they came? This light! This climate. The mountains and sea. And the food!" Pamela had planned an art day for us, including lunch at a hotel known for its art collection.

We started in Grasse for a whirlwind tour of the villa where one of my favorite painters, Jean-Honoré Fragonard, was born. We drove down to Vallauris, the village where Picasso lived, to see his powerful depiction of war and peace on the walls of a chapel and to buy some Picasso-inspired clay pots. Then we drove north to Saint-Paul-de-Vence, where Chagall lived, to have lunch at La Colombe d'Or, the hotel whose owner encouraged artists to trade their art for food and lodging. Strolling first through the garden to see the Leget ceramic mural and by the pool to see the Calder, Pamela decided to sprawl glamorously across the pillows in the sunken bar area with a glass of wine, while I took a self-guided tour of the art collection on the walls. Our lunch was excellent, from the old-world service to the delicate salmon *quenelles*, the *pavé de bœuf*, and puffy soufflés Grand Marnier. This bohemian paradise, where Picasso, Matisse, Chagall, and so many others had dined, was our haven for a couple of magical hours.

Later we took a walk to work off our meal, up a hill to Saint Claire church to see Chagall's painting *Couple on Top of Saint Paul*, which captures the mood of the Riviera and its golden light. We walked back by Chagall's house then, reenergized, and hopped into the car to drive a few moments over to Vence to visit the chapel whose interior was painted by Matisse when he lived there. Our day ended in Cagnes-sur-Mer, visiting Renoir's beautiful home and studio.

Pamela, still full of life, called out to me as she dropped me off at home, "But there's more! We must do this again! There's the Marc Chagall Museum in Nice with over three hundred of his paintings and . . .!" I couldn't wait for our next art adventure.

Back to the food! Our meal at Colombe d'Or gave me the impetus to make a large piece of beef like the one I had at lunch, for my husband's birthday. After consulting with the butcher, I came away with beautiful bone-in rib steaks to roast according to his directions. To complete the meal, I placed them on thick toasts the way my grandmother used to serve steaks, to catch the juices. I also had the butcher slice long marrowbones vertically to roast and serve alongside.

This is a superb cut of meat, perfect for a special meal. Each steak should serve two people.

Tip: Chef Pierre Gagnaire offers a recipe where he flames a bunch of thyme to infuse the beef with its aroma while roasting. You can add a smoking thyme bunch in the oven for an added layer of flavor.

Serves 4

2 (1 1/2 to 2-inch thick) bone-in rib steaks, room temperature (preferably aged)

6 tablespoons extra virgin olive oil, divided, plus more for brushing

2 beef marrowbones, 3–5 inches long, sliced vertically

   sea salt

1 bunch thyme, tied with kitchen twine (optional)

4 slices bread, cut 1 inch thick

1 large clove garlic, halved

1 crusty baguette, sliced

   fleur de sel

   freshly ground black pepper

   Dijon mustard

Preheat oven to 400 degrees F.

Pat the meat dry with paper towels.

Use two ovenproof skillets. Heat 3 tablespoons oil in each skillet until shimmering hot, then place a steak in each. Do not season the steaks and do not be tempted to move them. You want to sear them brown on both sides. Turn them over after 3 minutes, and sear the other side about 3 minutes.

Meanwhile, place the marrowbones on a baking pan with sides and sprinkle with sea salt. Move the baking pan and both steaks in their skillets to the hot oven. *Note:* If you are going to use a bundle of thyme, flame it then blow out the flame so that it is still smoking; add it to one of the steak skillets in the oven.

Roast the steaks for about 10 minutes, or until a meat thermometer registers 140 degrees F. The meat will be rare but will continue cooking once out of the oven to about 145 degrees F., or medium-rare. Remove the steaks from the oven, cover loosely with a tent of aluminum foil, and allow them to rest for 8 minutes.

Leave the marrowbones in the oven, turn up the heat to 450 degrees F., and cook them for another 10 to 15 minutes (for a total cook time of 25 minutes). Watch them carefully, and if you see the marrow dissolving and leaking out into the pan, remove them from the oven and soak up the dissolved marrow with a couple of slices of the baguette to serve on the side.

Meanwhile, rub the 4 slices of bread with the cut side of the garlic, brush them with olive oil, sprinkle with a little sea salt, and place in the oven with the bones for 5 to 8 minutes, until they are warm and starting to turn golden.

When you are ready to carve the steaks, hold your knife parallel to the bone and cut each steak into 2 pieces.

To serve, place a slice of toasted bread on each plate and top with a piece of beef. Place a marrow-bone on one side, with a small bowl of fleur de sel, a pepper grinder, and a small bowl of Dijon mustard nearby. Serve with sliced baguette.

Hotel La Colombe d'Or
Place de Gualle
06570 Saint-Paul-de-Vence
Telephone: (33) 04 93 32 80 02
www.la-colombe-dor.com

LAMB STEW WITH ARTICHOKES, STRING BEANS, AND LIME
Le Ragoût d'Agneau aux Artichauts, aux Haricots Verts et au Citron Vert

There's a parallel universe that exists below the tables of French restaurants and cafés, where well-behaved dogs conduct conversations with their eyes. They are welcome, trained from an early age to slip under the table, settle down, and be quiet, knowing that as a reward for their good behavior their owners will discretely pass down tasty morsels after the meal.

Although most of the dogs are small in comparison to the black Labrador guide dogs I was training, cafés and bistros had no problem with my bringing them along with me for lunch to educate them so they could learn how to accompany their future owners, who might want to go out for a meal.

But beforehand, I had to train them at home. The best way I found to do it was to cook food they favored, because if they really wanted a taste, it was easier to condition them to sit quietly under the table while we ate. Once they were rewarded, they seemed to understand what was expected of them. This recipe was as big a hit with the wonderful dogs that passed through our lives as it was with us.

P.S. We fed them morsels of only the lamb for a treat, as onions are not good for dogs.

Serves 4-6

FOR THE MARINADE

$1/4$ cup olive oil

4 cloves garlic, sliced

2 shallots, minced

1 tablespoon rosemary leaves, minced

3 tablespoons lemon juice

1 teaspoon salt

FOR THE STEW

3 pounds lamb shoulder, cut into 2-inch pieces

1 cup flour

4 tablespoons olive oil

3 cups water

1 chicken bouillon cube

2 onions, finely chopped

4 carrots, grated

1 pound string beans, sliced into 1-inch pieces

1 can artichoke hearts, drained, sliced in half

2 limes, thinly sliced, plus 1 lime sliced thinly for garnish

salt

freshly ground black pepper

In a bowl, whisk together $1/4$ cup olive oil, garlic, shallots, rosemary, lemon juice, and salt. Pour into a large ziplock bag, add the lamb pieces, zip the bag shut, and move the lamb around to coat with the marinade. Refrigerate overnight.

Remove the lamb the next day, reserving the marinade, then dry each piece of lamb well on paper towels. Dredge pieces in flour.

Heat 4 tablespoons olive oil in a large heavy pot on medium heat. In batches, add the floured lamb pieces and brown on all sides. When browned, remove to a plate. Continue in batches, adding more oil if needed, until all have been browned and moved to the plate. Add 3 cups water to the pot and deglaze by running a spatula over the bottom to bring up the browned bits. Add the reserved marinade, bouillon cube, onions, carrots, and lamb and simmer for 1 hour, or until the lamb is tender.

Add the string beans, artichoke hearts, the 2 thinly sliced limes, and cook for another 15 minutes. Taste and adjust salt and pepper if needed. Garnish the stew with more small pieces of lime, and side it with a salad.

ORANGE BITTERS

Orange bitters is a flavoring made from bitter oranges, spices like coriander, cumin, caraway, sugar, and alcohol. There are a number of brands available in stores as well as online. Primarily used for cocktails, a couple of drops of orange bitters added before serving soup, stews, or dishes like this one adds an intriguing final top note of citrus.

"To Catch a Thief" Braised Pork
Le Porc Braisé au "Pour Attraper un Voleur"

Frances Stevens: "Would you like a leg or a breast?"

It was a stormy Sunday. I felt like cooking something big and hearty, but I also wanted to snuggle down in our deep, pillow-soft sofa and watch a video, Alfred Hitchcock's *To Catch a Thief*, which starred Grace Kelley and Cary Grant as amorous cat burglars on the Côte d'Azur, circa the 1950s. What could I make that would let us watch the movie yet would result in an after-movie dinner that we could enjoy with candle light and a good bottle of wine?

I decided on this braised pork and served it over tender egg noodles with a drizzle of orange bitters for a crazy but deliriously delicious final touch. I was able to watch *To Catch a Thief*, thrill at the driving scenes along the narrow coastal road from Nice to Monaco, cheer, and cry, and was still able to make a delectable meal. So whenever I want to do something else on a Sunday, I put this dish in the oven to cook and enjoy the free time. Braised pork is almost effortless, seemingly cooking itself, and it's perfectly timed for a movie!

Unlike a daube, where the pieces of meat are cut into smaller pieces, this is made with large pieces of pork that are braised until fall-apart tender. The traditional Niçoise recipe adds chopped capers and gherkins to the sauce. Once you make this version, you can add in capers, gherkins, or whole small mushrooms, if you wish, when you add the fresh herbs at the end.

Serves 4

2 pounds boneless pork shoulder,
   sliced into 4 pieces

   sea salt

   freshly ground black pepper

5 tablespoons extra virgin
   olive oil, divided

1 onion, chopped

4 large cloves garlic, chopped

2 cups dry white wine, plus more
   for topping up during braising

1 cup chicken broth

3 carrots, sliced into bite-size pieces

2 stalks celery, including leaves, chopped

1 fennel bulb, sliced; fronds
   chopped for garnish

4 bay leaves

2 tablespoons fresh thyme
   leaves, divided

2 fresh sage leaves, torn into pieces

   Cooked noodles

   fleur de sel

Tie each piece of pork around the perimeter with a piece of kitchen twine, then salt and pepper each side.

Preheat the oven to 300 degrees F.

Heat 3 tablespoons olive oil in a Dutch oven or heavy pot that has a lid until it is shimmering hot. Add the pieces of pork and sear each side until golden brown. Remove the pork to a plate, pour off any fat from the pot and discard.

Add 2 tablespoons oil to the pot and cook the onion and garlic for 3 minutes.

Pour in 2 cups wine and chicken broth, return the pork pieces to the pot, cover, place in the oven, and braise for 1 hour. Add the carrots, celery, sliced fennel, and bay leaves, and cook for 1 more hour. Add 1 tablespoon thyme leaves, sage leaves, and salt and pepper to taste, and cook for another $1/2$ hour, until fork tender. *Note:* if the liquid drops to below halfway up the pork, top up with wine to reach $3/4$ of the way up the meat.

Remove pork from the oven to a plate, and discard the bay leaves that are in the braising sauce. Taste the sauce for seasoning, adding salt and pepper if needed.

Heap cooked noodles on each plate, top with a piece of pork, then ladle the braising sauce over each piece of pork. Garnish with remaining thyme leaves and chopped fennel fronds. Serve with a small bowl of fleur de sel and set a pepper grinder nearby for coarse grinding.

SALT COD STEW
L'Estocaficada

The Niçoise fish stew called *estocaficada* is made with stockfish, a local ingredient difficult to find elsewhere. This version substitutes its cousin, the milder salt cod. For good salt cod, look for the ones that come from Norway, which are white. If you find salt cod that is in little pieces and looks yellow, it's better to use large pieces of fresh cod, which I often do.

Serves 4

2 pounds salt cod

3 tablespoons extra virgin olive oil, plus more to drizzle

5 cloves garlic, sliced

3 tablespoons chopped flat leaf parsley

6 anchovies, minced

3 cups dry white wine

4 large onions, chopped

4 large leeks, cleaned and sliced thinly

2 carrots, finely chopped

   fresh thyme and parsley leaves

3 pounds small potatoes (e.g., fingerlings or new), halved or quartered

2 bell peppers, green, red, or orange, chopped

3 pounds tomatoes, chopped

1 can pitted black olives or oil-cured olives, drained, plus 14 whole Niçoise or black olives, pitted, for garnish

2 tablespoons Cognac

   salt

   freshly ground black pepper

3 tablespoons finely chopped fresh basil

16 cherry tomatoes, coarsely chopped

1 crusty baguette

Rinse the salt cod well under running water, then soak it in cold water, covered, in the refrigerator for 24 hours, changing the water three times. If you can find pre-soaked salt cod, eliminate this step. Pick out any visible bones and pat dry. Slice into small chunks. If using fresh cod, rinse, pat dry, and leave in large pieces.

In a soup pot, heat the olive oil and sauté the garlic and parsley for 3 minutes. Add the cod and sauté for 4 minutes. Add the anchovies and sauté for 5 minutes. Add the wine, bring to a boil, and simmer for 5 minutes. Add the onions, leeks, carrots, and the herbs and cook on medium heat for 15 minutes.

In the meantime, cook the potatoes in boiling water until just tender, then drain.

Add the potatoes, bell peppers, chopped tomatoes, and olives to the soup pot and cook for another 10 minutes. Add water if you would like more broth in your stew.

Pour in the Cognac and stir well. Taste and adjust salt and pepper as desired.

Serve the stew with a drizzle of olive oil over the top. Garnish with olives, chopped basil, and cherry tomatoes, and serve with a warm crusty baguette.

sweet endings

Les Desserts

THE CHEESE PLATE
Le Plateau de Fromages

If you walk into almost any French kitchen you will find the makings of a cheese plate—the course that appears after salad and before dessert, or in place of dessert. Served with good bread and wine, it blesses the end of a meal with a final note of *joie de vivre*.

Choosing cheeses is a highly personal ritual, reflective of whether you buy your favorites or choose to offer your family and guests an interesting variety based on starting with a traditional progression from mild cheese and ending with the most pungent. In this case, asking the *fromager* what is ripe and perfect for serving at that moment yields a never-ending variety of cheeses.

When you find a good cheese shop, it is the *affineur* who has curated the selection, aged the cheeses, and made sure they are only offered for sale when they have reached their peak. The *fromagerie* I normally buy my cheese from is Fromagerie Ceneri, on rue Meynadier in Cannes, where the father and son *affineurs* present more than 250 cheeses and take pride in educating my palate. I make the trip there once a week for a selection that I can serve every night. My cheese board displays our favorite cheeses—a fresh local organic cheese from the little Alpine *chamoisée* goats at La Ferme des Courmettes in Tourrettes-sur-Loup; a creamy Boursault; the mild Bleu d'Auvergne; Roquefort; a Brie de Meaux; a Gruyère—and always includes an aromatic Époisses, plus one or two others recommended by the *affineur*.

For special occasions, I add a runny Vacherin and serve it with a spoon. Sometimes, I set out a slab of unsalted butter with a shower of fleur de sel on top, because I can't imagine eating good bread without it.

PEACH AND RASPBERRY SALAD WITH DARK CHOCOLATE SORBET

La Salade de Pêches et Framboises Garni de Sorbet au Chocolat Noir

On hot summer nights, sliced peaches mingled with raspberries and topped with homemade deep chocolate sorbet that begins to seep over the fruit is a crowd pleaser — especially if the peaches and raspberries are very ripe.

Be generous when you serve it, filling bowls to the top with fruit and at least two scoops of sorbet. You will need an ice cream machine.

Serves 4-6

FOR THE CHOCOLATE SORBET

3/4 cups plus 2 tablespoons sugar

3/4 cup unsweetened cocoa powder, sifted

pinch of salt

2 1/4 cups water

1 tablespoon corn syrup

3 ounces semisweet chocolate, finely chopped

1/2 teaspoon vanilla extract

2 teaspoons instant espresso powder

FOR THE FRUIT

1/2 cup sugar

1 star anise, broken

1/2 cup water

1 tablespoon orange flower water

8 fresh ripe peaches

2 pints fresh raspberries

Pre-freeze the bowl and paddle of your ice cream machine overnight.

Place the sugar, cocoa powder, salt, water, and corn syrup in a medium saucepan and whisk well to blend. Bring to a boil and cook for 1 minute, whisking all the while.

Remove from the heat; add the chopped chocolate, vanilla, and espresso powder. Whisk to blend, allowing the chocolate bits to melt, and continue whisking until smooth. Let cool to room temperature, cover with plastic wrap, and refrigerate for 1 hour.

Remove the paddle and ice cream machine bowl from the freezer. Pour the chilled chocolate mixture into the bowl and turn on the machine. Sorbet should take 40 to 45 minutes.

Transfer frozen sorbet to a covered freezer container and freeze for 4 hours or overnight.

Make the syrup for the peaches by putting the sugar, star anise, and 1/2 cup water in a saucepan. Bring to a boil and stir until the sugar is dissolved; then remove from the heat, cover, and allow to cool to room temperature. Strain through a fine sieve into a bowl; discard the star anise. Stir in the orange flower water.

Peel the peaches over another bowl to catch the juices. Slice them into the bowl, pour the sugar syrup over the top, toss, and refrigerate while the sorbet is freezing.

To serve, chill serving bowls; place the peaches with their juice into the bowls. Spoon juice from the bottom of the bowl the peaches were in over the top. Then add the fresh raspberries and scoops of chocolate sorbet.

Note: For a winter version of this recipe, use pink grapefruit, pears, apples, or oranges.

Frozen Fresh Fig Mousse
with White Wine Caramel Sauce
La Mousse Glacée aux Figues Fraîches, Sauce Caramel au Vin Blanc

It's as if a miracle happened while I was standing in front of the cathedral. I found Fenocchio.

Totally by chance, I gazed across the square, saw a long line of people, and made my way there to see what everyone was waiting for.

The miracle was that I am passionate about ice cream—really good ice cream—and since I was new to Nice, I had yet to discover where to go. My prayers were answered.

Imagine reading ice cream labels like the following: pine nuts and preserved mandarins, tomato basil, licorice, lavender, beer, rose, jasmine, cactus, walnut, avocado, vanilla with whole almonds, candied ginger, chili chocolate—more than a hundred fresh flavors are made there every day.

My first cone was enough to make me a devotee. Never was there a trip to Nice after that without a visit to Fenocchio.

I later read that Catherine de Medici, when she learned she was to leave Italy and marry Henry II of France, took recipes and chefs with her to make sorbets and iced desserts when she passed through the Côte d'Azur on her way to her wedding in Marseille. I like to think she would have loved Fenocchio.

I make a lot of ice cream and sorbets at home, and when my fig trees are overflowing with fruit, I make this fig ice cream with a delicious caramel sauce. It doesn't need an ice cream machine. The only thing you have to remember is to make it the day before you want to serve it. Pour it into a freezer container or a loaf pan lined with plastic wrap. If you use a freezer container, scoop it out and serve with the sauce. If you freeze it in a loaf pan, serve it in slices with a pool of sauce around it.

Serves 8

FOR THE FIG MIXTURE

10 ripe black figs

1/3 cup sugar

1 1/2 teaspoons almond extract

1 teaspoon vanilla extract

FOR THE MOUSSE

6 large egg yolks, beaten

1 cup heavy cream, plus 2 cups chilled heavy cream

2 tablespoons all-purpose flour

1 cup milk

1/2 cup honey

1/4 cup sugar

1 teaspoon almond extract

1/2 teaspoon vanilla extract

FOR THE WINE CARAMEL SAUCE

1 1/4 cup tightly packed light brown sugar

1/2 cup white sugar

1 cup water

1/4 cup corn syrup

3 teaspoons vanilla extract

1/2 cup heavy cream

1 cup dry white wine (or port or Madeira)

1 tablespoon salted butter

Wash the figs and remove the stems; finely chop. Place them in a large saucepan over low heat with the sugar and almond and vanilla extracts. Stir and cook until the mixture thickens enough that you will be able to swirl it through the mousse. Remove from the heat.

Place a large bowl filled halfway with water and ice cubes nearby.

To prepare the mousse, heat water in a double boiler or pot to simmering; do not let it boil. Put the egg yolks, 1 cup heavy cream, flour, milk, honey, sugar, and almond and vanilla extracts in a smaller pan. Whisk to combine, and then place the small pan over the simmering hot water. Whisk while the mixture cooks for about 13 to 15 minutes, or until it thickens and coats the back of a wooden spoon. At the end, set the pan directly over the heat, whisking vigorously to get the custard for the mousse as thick as possible.

Immediately remove the pan from the heat and lower into the ice water bath to cool the custard. When cool, cover the pan and refrigerate for 30 minutes.

Line a freezer container or loaf pan with plastic wrap.

When the custard is cold, beat 2 cups chilled heavy cream until it reaches soft peaks (not stiff). Fold one-third into the custard until mixed; then gently fold in the rest until just blended. Pour mousse into prepared freezer container.

Drizzle the fig mixture in a stream over the top, and with a knife swirl it down into the mousse. Cover with plastic wrap and freeze overnight.

To make the wine caramel sauce, put the sugars, water, corn syrup, and vanilla in a heavy saucepan. Stir with a wooden spoon, then bring to a boil. When a candy thermometer reaches 290 degrees F., stir again. When it reaches 340 degrees F., remove from heat and very carefully pour in the heavy cream, standing back, as it may spatter. Then add in the white wine, stir, and cook for 2 minutes. . Refrigerate until ready to use.

Just before serving the frozen mousse, warm the sauce and whisk in the butter until it looks glossy. Spoon the warm wine caramel sauce around the frozen mousse.

Fenocchio Maître Glacier
2 place Rossetti
06300 Nice
Telephone: (33) 04 93 80 72 52
www.fenocchio.fr

Giant Mocha Meringues
Les Meringues de Moka

Many of the bakeries in Nice and along the coast bake giant meringues. I buy mine in a bakery in Cannes, then make a silly mess of myself as I eat them while walking around and end up with meringue snow cascading down the front of me.

The playful mounds of meringue are irresistible and beautiful swirled with flavorings like almond, raspberry, chocolate, or lemon.

For the cost of a dozen eggs, you can make them at home, ending up with spectacular looking sweets children will love and adults will gasp over. Once you make the basic recipe, you can tailor it for adult appeal, adding instant espresso and cocoa swirls or rum-soaked raisins and cinnamon. I make dark chocolate meringues for New Year's and splurge on culinary gold leaf to decorate them. To make some with children in mind, try adding orange, Nutella, or chocolate chips and chopped nuts.

Makes 8-10 cookies

2   tablespoons unsweetened cocoa

2   tablespoons Medaglia D'Oro Instant Espresso Coffee powder

12   large egg whites, room temperature

3   cups sugar

1/2 teaspoon almond extract

     pinch of salt

     pinch of cream of tartar

Arrange oven shelves to allow for maximum height above both shelves. Line 2 large baking pans with parchment paper.

Sift together the cocoa and espresso powder into a bowl.

Put the egg whites, sugar, almond extract, salt, and cream of tartar in a large saucepan over low heat; and stir continually. Put a candy thermometer into the pan, and when the egg whites reach 99 degrees F., about 4 to 5 minutes, take the pan off the heat and pour the egg white mixture into the bowl of a stand mixer. Beat the whites until they are stiff and can hold their shape, about 8 minutes. It may take longer, depending on the weather and other variables. (If you are using an electric hand mixer, it will take quite a bit longer. Just keep beating until they are very glossy and stiff and hold their shape.)

Preheat the oven to 230 degrees F.

Using a big serving spoon, scoop a large amount to make a giant cookie and place it on the baking pan. You can pile them high. Continue to make large cookies, leaving an inch or two between for expansion as they cook. Sieve the espresso and cocoa powder over the top of the cookies, then use a knife to swirl it through each one.

Place in the oven to bake for 1 hour. Rotate the pans (turn them), then bake for another 30 to 60 minutes, until the cookies are crisp on the outside and still chewy on the inside. The time it takes to cook them depends on the size of the meringues. If they feel firm when you touch them and are no longer sticky, they are ready to take out of the oven.

Cool cookies for 15 minutes on the baking trays, then transfer to a cooling rack. Cool completely before eating. The cookies will keep in an airtight container for two days.

ANISE COOKIES
Les Navettes d'Anise

When Lilly graduated, I wept. She was one of the last guide dog puppies I nurtured at home, and I always worried for her because she was such a delicate, sweet little girl, I wanted only the best match for her. I took her down to Biot for graduation to gift her to the blind person waiting to take her home. It was always an emotional affair, but this time it seemed harder.

My husband and I got in the car with Lilly, and I held her on the way. When we walked her through the gate to the school, a large group of people were already seated, waiting for the ceremony. I reluctantly released her leash, giving it to someone who led her up to join the other puppies on the podium. We took our seats. When our turn came, we walked up and stood with Lilly while an adorable thirteen-year-old girl came forward with her mother. I admit it was very hard. But when I saw her sweet face and the gentleness of her trembling hands on Lilly's head, my heart leapt for joy—for both of them.

A year later a Christmas card arrived. It was a picture of Lilly and her little girl, standing by the sea in Normandy. Lilly looked absolutely fine. The little girl looked radiant.

I made these cookies for Lilly's graduation party, and they are the ones I sent to the little girl for her first Christmas with gentle Lilly. They are my version of the ones made at Lou Canice, in old town Nice. They are called *navettes*, made in the shape of a small oval, and are flavored with orange blossom water, rose water, lavender, or anise. Orange flower navettes are associated with Marseilles, but in Nice at Lou Canice, you find them made with anise seeds. They taste entirely different, entirely Niçoise.

Makes 12 cookies

1   tablespoon anise seeds

1   cup all-purpose flour

¼   cup sugar

½   teaspoon salt

¼   cup unsalted butter, room temperature

2   egg yolks

1   teaspoon anise extract

½   teaspoon vanilla extract

1   tablespoon plus a few drops of
    water to hold dough together

    confectioners' sugar

In a food processor, pulse the anise seeds until they are finely chopped. Scoop the seeds into a bowl; add the flour, sugar, salt, and whisk to blend.

With an electric mixer, beat the butter until fluffy, then add the egg yolks one by one and beat well. Add the anise and vanilla extracts and beat to incorporate.

Add the wet ingredients to the dry ingredients and mix with a wooden spoon. If the dough is too dry, add the water until you can get the dough to come together when you pinch it with your fingers. Scoop it out onto a sheet of plastic wrap, bring together into a ball, and chill in the refrigerator for 3 hours.

Preheat the oven to 350 degrees F. Line a baking sheet with parchment paper.

On a clean, floured work surface, work the dough into a long roll. Slice off 2-inch pieces. Manipulate each piece into an oval shape with tapered ends and make a slight slice down the middle.

Place the navettes on the baking sheet, and bake for 8 to 15 minutes, until they are golden brown. The timing depends on how long and thick you shaped your cookies. Allow them to cool, then sprinkle with confectioners' sugar and serve.

Note: If you have coarse sugar crystals, sprinkling some on top before baking yields a delightfully crunchy crust.

Lou Canice
7 bis rue Mascoinat
06300 Nice
Telephone: (33) 04 93 85 41 62
www.Facebook.com/Lou-Canice

Honey Spice Loaf from Gourdon
Le Pain d'Épice de Gourdon

The road curves then straightens out, then curves, climbing so steeply that you have to keep the steering wheel to the left for several minutes as you circle and circle upwards. After parking, you walk up a road that climbs steeply to the top of the hill for a panoramic view of mountains, valleys, and the coast, which includes paragliders criss-crossing the air in front of your eyes.

This is Gourdon, one of the famed perched villages of the Côte d'Azur, which on a moonless night looks like a brightly lit space ship hovering in the sky above my house. In terms of gastronomic delights, the steep hairpin road leading up to it is worth navigating for Gourdon's famous *pain d'epices*—a simple loaf cake made all over France. In Gourdon, these cakes are unique in that they are baked with the zest from local bitter oranges, or local candied fruits, and a generous amount of local mountain honey gathered by Gourdon shopkeepers.

Without traveling to Gourdon, it can be baked at home, filling the air with the scent of spices and honey. Serve it warm with a dollop of whipped cream and a drizzle of honey or bittersweet chocolate sauce. Pain d'epices is also delicious toasted, with butter, spread with honey, and topped with soft goat cheese; or paired with savories like smoked salmon or foie gras.

Makes 1 loaf, or 12 slices

1 cup water

½ cup fresh orange juice, plus zest from 1 organic orange

2 teaspoons dark rum

1 teaspoon anise extract

1 cup dark brown sugar

1 ½ cups liquid honey (nice with buckwheat honey)

2 cups all-purpose flour

2 cups dark rye flour

2 teaspoons baking soda

½ teaspoon salt

1 tablespoon anise seeds

1 tablespoon ground cinnamon

½ teaspoon ground cloves

1 teaspoon freshly grated nutmeg

1 large egg, plus 1 egg yolk, beaten

Heavily butter a 9 x 5 x 3 loaf pan and coat with sugar. Tap out excess sugar.

Preheat the oven to 350 degrees F.

Put the water, juice, rum, anise extract, sugar, and honey in a saucepan. Cook until the sugar is dissolved. Take off the heat and allow to cool a little, yet still remain liquid.

In a large bowl, whisk together the dry ingredients and spices to blend. Pour in the honey mixture, as well as the eggs and orange zest, and mix well to blend.

Pour the batter into the loaf pan and bake for 1 hour, until a cake tester comes out clean. Check after 45 minutes, and if the top is becoming too brown, cover loosely with a piece of aluminum foil for the rest of the baking time.

Cool to room temperature before removing from the pan.

Madame's Peaches and Cream Tart
La Tarte de Madame aux Pêches et à la Crème

My first weeks learning how to cook local cuisine with Madame up the hill were spent baking. One of my favorite lessons was this peaches and cream tart, which I am not sure can be claimed to be authentically Niçoise but which I know came from her mother's hand-written notes, that were laid out on the table as we cooked.

We made the tart, then sat down and ate half of it warm, right out of the oven. A pot of tea was always part of our baking ritual, along with a wee little glass of homemade orange liqueur that Monsieur would pour for us; then he would disappear.

Serves 8

1 stick unsalted butter, room temperature

2 cups all-purpose flour

3/4 cup sugar, divided, plus 2 tablespoons

7 peaches, unpeeled, sliced thickly or quartered

2 eggs

1 teaspoon vanilla extract

1 teaspoon almond extract

1 cup heavy cream

Preheat oven to 400 degrees F. Butter and flour a 9-inch pie plate or a tart pan with a removable bottom.

In a bowl, beat the butter until fluffy. Add the flour and 1/4 cup sugar, and work with your hands until it comes together into a dough. Press dough into the pie plate or tart pan.

Lay the peaches, cut side up, in a decorative pattern in the pie plate. Sprinkle with 1/2 cup sugar.

Bake at 400 degrees F. for 20 minutes.

Beat the eggs with 1 tablespoon sugar and vanilla and almond extracts. Whisk in the heavy cream and pour all on top of the peaches. Sprinkle with remaining 1 tablespoon sugar and return to the oven. Bake for 30 minutes, until the top is golden brown. Allow to cool and set before serving.

NUTELLA ORANGE AND RUM MOUSSE
La Mousse de Nutella, Orange et Rhum

The northwest region of Italy that borders France—the Piedmont—is famous for producing Nutella, so Nice naturally shares many dishes as well as a common love for Nutella. Anywhere you can buy a warm crêpe in Nice, you will find it stuffed with melting Nutella. Everyone has a jar on the shelf, ready to stir into cocoa, spread on toast, or slather on cake. It's also excellent blended into the following chocolate mousse.

Serves 6

10	ounces semisweet chocolate chips
5	eggs, yolks and whites separated, room temperature
1/2	cup Nutella
2	teaspoons orange zest
2	ounces dark rum
1 3/4	cups heavy cream, cold
1	teaspoon vanilla extract
1	cup chopped hazelnuts

Place the chips in a double boiler over simmering water and stir until they are melted and glossy. Transfer the chocolate to a large bowl and stir in egg yolks with a wooden spoon, one at a time, until well blended. Then stir in the Nutella, orange zest, and rum. (If the chocolate seizes up, return it to the double boiler and whisk over simmering water until the mixture is melted again and glossy. Remove from the heat.)

Beat the egg whites until they hold stiff peaks. Fold one-third of the whites into the chocolate mixture. When it is well blended, fold in the remaining two-thirds.

Beat the cream and vanilla until almost stiff, then fold one-third into the chocolate mixture until well blended. Fold in the remaining whipped cream until blended.

Spoon into individual bowls or one large serving bowl. Start with a layer of mousse, then a layer of hazelnuts, and top with mousse. Cover with plastic wrap and chill at least 3 hours. Garnish with chopped hazelnuts.

This mousse freezes well and can be served like ice cream.

ALMOND-ORANGE POLENTA SQUARES
Estouffadou Niçois

"The discovery of a new dish does more for human happiness than the discovery of a new star." — Brillat-Savarin

An elusive treat, these soft polenta squares sometimes pop up in stalls in the open-air market in Nice and sometimes in small bakeries; and sometimes they are hard to find when you wish you could. When I discovered *estouffadou Niçoise*, the plainest and most unpromising-looking sweet, I felt yet again the happiness of coming upon a new dish that I had never heard of or tasted before in my quest to learn traditional recipes from the area around Nice.

The sign above read, *"Estouffadou Niçois: polenta, amande, sucre, beurre."* A relatively thin cake in a large metal pan, it was cut into squares flecked with ground almonds and sporting a beguiling crunchiness from the polenta. Every time I found one, I tried it. Some were grainy like the first one I tried; some were soft pillows that melted in your mouth; yet all had the same sugar-butter-almond flavor. Because they were hard to find, I worked on a recipe and came up with one that produces a soft, moist cake, with texture from the ground almonds and perfume from the orange peel.

Makes 16

1 cup whole almonds

1 cup all-purpose flour

1 3/4 cups cornmeal

1 1/2 teaspoons baking powder

1/2 teaspoon salt

1 stick unsalted butter, room temperature

1 cup sugar

1 teaspoon vanilla extract

1 1/2 teaspoons almond extract

1 large organic orange, zested and juiced

3 large eggs

1/2 cup milk

Heat the oven to 350 degrees F. Butter a 10-inch-square baking pan, then place a buttered piece of parchment paper in the bottom.

Place the almonds on a baking sheet and bake for 6 minutes, until lightly golden brown. Remove from the oven and cool completely, then process in a food processor until finely ground.

In a large bowl, whisk together the flour, cornmeal, baking powder, salt, and ground almonds.

Using a stand mixer, beat the butter until light and fluffy, about 3 minutes. Add the sugar and beat. Add both extracts, the orange zest, and 3/4 cup orange juice; mix to combine. Beat in the eggs, one by one, until well blended, then beat in the milk.

Fold the dry ingredients into the wet ingredients. Pour into the prepared baking pan and bake for 25 to 30 minutes, until golden on top. Allow to rest for 15 minutes before slicing.

To serve, slice into squares, or into 2-inch-wide long strips that you then slice on the diagonal to produce individual one-bite cakes. They are delicious plain or showered with a light dusting of confectioners' sugar for decoration, and the squares make a delightful bed for sliced strawberries with whipped cream.

Note: Estouffadou also makes a great base for hors d'oeuvres, sliced into small squares and topped with a cube of cheese or a swath of smoked salmon or ham.

Sweet Carnival Fritters
Les Ganses

At carnival time in Nice, before the fasting begins for Lent, you can find delicate *ganses*, a fried dough flavored with orange flower water and dusted with confectioners' sugar. These appear in bakeries and at restaurants and cafés under the name *ganses* or *bugnes*. If you happen to dance late into the night and stroll over to the beach to cool off and watch the stars, you might be rewarded with the appearance of someone selling freshly made *ganses* from a basket slung over their arm. That's when life feels really good.

Try this recipe and discover how quickly they are made and how very light and delicate they are.

Makes 30

3   cups all-purpose flour plus
    3 tablespoons, divided

1   teaspoon salt

3/4 cup sugar

2   tablespoons orange zest

1   stick unsalted butter, cold

2   tablespoons orange blossom water

1   teaspoon vanilla extract

4   eggs, room temperature

    vegetable oil for frying

    confectioners' sugar for garnish

    finely grated orange peel, optional

To the bowl of a food processor, add 3 cups flour, salt, sugar, and orange zest; pulse 5 times. Slice in the butter and pulse 5 times.

Pour the orange blossom water, vanilla, and eggs into a separate bowl, and whisk until blended. Add egg mixture to the food processor and process until a dough ball forms. If the dough is too sticky, add 1 tablespoon flour and process again. Repeat if necessary.

Scoop the dough onto a large piece of plastic wrap, wrap tightly, and refrigerate for 1 hour.

Flour a clean work surface. Divide dough into 6 balls. With a rolling pin, roll out each ball very thinly, adding more flour to the work surface and rolling pin as needed.

With a pizza cutter or knife, cut into strips 1/2 to 1 1/2 inches wide, then into 1 1/2-inch pieces. Or cut into random shapes. (The traditional method is to make a slit in the middle of each strip and slip one end of the dough through the slit to form a "knot.")

Heat about 1/2 inch of oil in a deep, wide pan. When the temperature reaches 325 degrees F., begin dropping in the dough pieces, a few at a time. Fry in batches until just golden on one side, then quickly flip and cook until just golden on the other side. Do not let them brown. Drain on paper towels.

Once all are cooked, put confectioners' sugar in a sieve and shake over the *ganses*. Then enjoy! Another way to present them is to finely grate more orange peel over them and shake the confectioners' sugar over the top.

NICE CARNIVAL

Dating back to 1294, the carnival in Nice is the oldest and biggest in France. Spectacular floats, fireworks, parties, street performers, and a battle of the flowers make it one of the best parties of the year. Theater, music, and dancing are part of the celebration, while street vendors sell local treats and restaurants create special menus for the event. And the best part? It lasts for ten days!

LIMONCELLO CAKE WITH TOWERING MERINGUE
Le Gâteau au Limoncello Meringué

"Lovely night, oh night of love,
Smile upon our joys,
Night much sweeter than the day
Oh beautiful night!
Time flies irretrievably
Wins our affections,
From this happy oasis,
*Time flies, no return."**

When I walked up the hill to visit Madame, I would hear this aria emanating from their house. As I got closer, *"Belle Nuit, O Nuit D'Amour"* would take hold of me, its swell of tender notes floating like tendrils out of the windows, pulling me forward.

One day, I pushed open the door to a crescendo of music. She was sitting in front of me on a hard chair, looking up at me with pleading, teary eyes. "I never got to say good-bye . . ."

After the funeral, we hugged and I said I'd stop by soon. The next week, I made her a cake. That's all I could do. Making something to eat was the way we comforted each other.

This is the cake I made for Madame. I wanted to bake something that would be a surprise. I opted for this American-size-and-shape cake. It would be unusual to find one that looked like this in France, and I thought it would create a diversion. It would be way too big for Madame to eat on her own, but hopefully it would prompt her to share it with her friends and bring some life into the house. She would always tell me, "Cook with love!" and I spent every minute making this cake with love in my heart.

*Madame and Monsieur's theme song, "Belle Nuit, O Nuit D'Amour," is an aria from *The Tales of Hoffman*, an opera by Jacques Offenbach.

Serves 8

FOR THE CAKE

2¾ cups cake flour

½ teaspoon salt

2 teaspoons baking powder

2 large eggs

1 cup light brown sugar

7 tablespoons unsalted butter, room temperature

rind of 1 organic lemon, coarsely grated on box grater

1 teaspoon vanilla extract

¼ cup vegetable oil

¾ cup milk, plus 2 tablespoons

2 tablespoons fresh lemon juice

½ cup Limoncello liqueur

4 large egg whites

½ cup granulated sugar

⅛ cup Limoncello liqueur, divided

FOR THE FROSTING

12 tablespoons (1 1/2 sticks) unsalted
 butter, room temperature

7 cups confectioners' sugar, sifted

1/4 cup milk

1 teaspoon vanilla extract

2 tablespoons fresh lemon juice

2 tablespoons Limoncello liqueur

1 tablespoons water, if needed

2 organic lemons, rind only,
 coarsely grated on box grater

FOR THE MERINGUE

1/2 cup granulated sugar (superfine is best)

6 egg whites, room temperature

1/2 teaspoon cream of tartar

1/2 teaspoon vanilla extract

Heat oven to 350 degrees F. Butter and flour two 9-inch round cake pans.

In a mixing bowl, add the flour, salt, and baking powder, and whisk to blend.

In a food processor, add the whole eggs and light brown sugar and process for 60 seconds. Add the butter, lemon rind, and vanilla and process for 60 seconds, scraping down the sides halfway through. Add the oil, milk, lemon juice, and 1/2 cup Limoncello, and process for 10 seconds. Add the dry ingredients and pulse 3 times.

With an electric beater, beat the 4 egg whites until almost stiff. Add 1/2 cup of granulated sugar and beat until egg whites hold their shape. Scoop them into the food processor and pulse just until they are mixed in.

Divide the batter between the pans and bake for 20 to 25 minutes, until a cake tester comes out clean. Cool in the pans for 12 minutes, then remove from pans.

Place one cake on a serving plate, slipping pieces of parchment paper under its bottom all the way around, then brush it with half of the 1/8 cup Limoncello and allow it to soak in before spreading with frosting.

To make the frosting, with an electric mixer, beat butter until fluffy. Beat in the confectioners' sugar, milk, vanilla, lemon juice, and Limoncello until smooth. If the frosting is too dry, add 1 tablespoon water and beat until spreadable. Beat in the lemon rind.

Frost the bottom cake layer, then set the second cake on top. Brush the top of the other cake layer with the remaining amount of 1/8 cup Limoncello, then frost the sides of the cake. (If you do not want to use meringue for a topping, you will have enough frosting to cover the top of the cake.)

To make the meringue topping, fill a saucepan halfway with water and bring to a simmer. Place sugar, egg whites, cream of tartar, and vanilla in a heatproof bowl, and whisk to blend. Set the bowl over the simmering water and whisk continually for 8 minutes, until the mixture is warm and the sugar is completely dissolved. Remove the bowl from the water.

With an electric beater or in a stand mixer, beat the mixture for 2 minutes on medium, then turn up to high speed and beat the meringue until glossy and very thick, about 15 minutes. It should be able to stand up on its own at this point.

Mound the meringue on top of the cake as high as you can, then make decorative swirls with a knife. Brown the meringue with a hand-held kitchen torch by gently passing it over the meringue in a circular motion.

Fruit Cake with Pistachios
Le "Cake" aux Fruits Confits à la Pistache

We were invited for dinner, so I stopped at a flower stall and bought a bouquet of yellow chrysanthemums, which they wrapped in clear cellophane with a long, trailing yellow satin ribbon. When our host answered the door, her eyes were huge; she covered her mouth and walked quickly away from us, only to be replaced by her husband, who at first had the same reaction, then laughed. He immediately explained that in France, bringing chrysanthemums to one's home was like bringing flowers to a grave—the message being that you don't wish the people well, but rather the opposite.

I've never since taken flowers when invited to dinner, especially not chrysanthemums, but rather made this sweet cake to contribute to the evening.

Makes 8-10 slices

½ cup salted shelled pistachios

½ cup mixed candied fruits or candied peel

2 cups all-purpose flour

½ teaspoon salt

1½ teaspoons baking powder

    zest of ½ organic orange

1 cup sugar

4 large eggs, beaten

1 teaspoon vanilla extract

¼ teaspoon almond extract

1 cup (2 sticks) unsalted butter, room temperature

2 tablespoons Grand Marnier, rum, or other liqueur, optional

2½ tablespoons orange or apricot marmalade, optional

Generously butter a 9 x 5 x 3-inch loaf pan; dust it with sugar on all sides and tap out the excess. Preheat the oven to 325 degrees F.

In a food processor, chop the pistachios; some will be finely ground and some in small pieces. Remove and reserve.

If the candied fruits are cut into a dice, they are ready to use. If not, chop them into small pieces.

Whisk the flour, salt, and baking powder in a bowl to combine.

Using a food processor, process the orange zest with the sugar for 30 seconds. Add in the eggs and extracts and process for 60 seconds. Thinly slice the butter into the work bowl, and process for another 60 seconds. Add the dry ingredients and pulse until they are just combined. The batter will be thick.

Scoop the batter out into a bowl, add the candied fruits and pistachios, and mix with a spoon until evenly incorporated. Scoop the batter into the loaf pan, and bake about 1 hour and 15 minutes, or until golden brown and a cake tester inserted into the center comes out clean. Remove from the oven and allow to cool for 5 minutes before taking the cake out of the pan.

Optional: Spoon the liqueur over the top of the cake while it is still warm. When it is cool, warm the marmalade in a pan and brush over the top. At this point you can decorate the top of the cake with candied fruits for a pretty garnish if you wish.

CANDIED FRUITS

Just down the road from my village is the small town of Pont-du-Loup, where Confiserie Florian manufactures their delectable fruits confits. A family business since 1949, Florian takes fresh local products—clementines from Vence, lemons from Menton, lemon verbena and Tango or Centifolia rose petals from Grasse, and violets picked the same day from Tourrettes-sur-Loup— and creates crystalized flowers, candied fruits, jams, caramels, and chocolates.

Confiserie Florian
06140 Le Pont-du-Loup
Telephone: (33) 04 93 59 32 91
www.confiserieflorian.com

Henri Auer, in Nice, is my other source for candied fruits and jams. Just steps away from the open-air market, Auer has been in operation since 1820 and is located in a store decorated in cream and gold, with a large crystal chandelier at its center. Shelves are brimming with fruits confits and jams, and at the back there is an area dedicated to their chocolates.

I can't resist leaving without a few marrons glacé or candied chestnuts, clementine jam, fig jam, and preserved ginger.

Maison Auer
7 Rue St. François-de-Paule
06300 Nice
Telephone: (33) 04 93 85 77 98
www.maison-auer.com

ABSINTHE MOUSSE WITH FENNEL FROND BRITTLE
La Mousse d'Absinthe, Croquant de Frondes de Fenouil

Madame's kitchen was bathed in soft olive greens and the strong yellow of the sunflowers growing just outside along her stone fence. The delicate fragrance of mimosas would waft through the open window when we baked.

Her life still revolved around her garden and making food. With Monsieur gone, she had more time to bake and to give me lessons. She still kept the two chairs that she and Monsieur used to sit in at night, facing the fireplace, so close they touched.

After a while, I graduated, and the following dessert is testament to the fact that I began branching out and experimenting on my own. Previously, she had walked down our hill to bring me sweets, but now it was me who walked up the hill with a bowl of absinthe mousse for her to try and bestow her blessing on.

Serves 4

1½ cups milk

1 cup sugar, plus 3 tablespoons

4 tablespoons all-purpose flour

3 large egg yolks, room temperature, beaten

3 tablespoons Absinthe liqueur, divided

1½ cups chilled heavy cream

FOR THE FENNEL BRITTLE

1 fennel bulb with fronds

2 cups sugar

3 tablespoons water

Prepare an ice water bath in a large bowl.

Heat water in a double boiler. In the top pot, add the milk, 1 cup sugar, flour, and yolks. Whisk constantly until it thickens, then switch to a wooden spoon, and when the mixture coats the back of the spoon, after about 13 minutes, add 2 tablespoons Absinthe. Remove from the heat and place the pot in the ice water bath to cool the custard. Refrigerate for 1 hour.

Whip the chilled cream until almost stiff, then beat in 3 tablespoons sugar and 1 tablespoon Absinthe. Gently fold half the whipped cream into the custard, then fold in the rest until just blended, taking care to keep the volume. Spoon into a large bowl or individual serving dishes, and refrigerate at least 4 hours, until ready to serve.*

If you would like to make fennel brittle as a garnish, remove the fronds from the fennel and keep the bulb for another use. Place parchment paper in a baking dish, and lay down the fennel fronds with their leaves spread out.

Bring sugar and water to a boil and allow to turn a dark caramel color, then carefully pour the hot caramel syrup over the top of the fennel fronds to coat. Allow to harden for 30 minutes, then with a knife or scissors, cut the brittle so that each piece has a frond in it. The brittle will look like glassy, transparent shards. Use to decorate the mousse before serving.

*Note: if you would rather serve it as an ice cream, this mixture is excellent frozen.

ABOUT ABSINTHE

The famous green-colored aperitif loved by Parisian artists and writers, such as Henri de Toulouse-Lautrec, Ernest Hemingway, Vincent Van Gogh, Charles Baudelaire, and Oscar Wilde, was banned from production in France because it allegedly caused hallucinations as well as other ills. It became so popular at one point that the hour when people would go to cafés to drink it, around 5 pm, was called "l'heure vert," the green hour.

Although its effects were never proven, its demise was replaced by Pastis, an aperitif with the same anise flavor but without the wormwood herb or chemical compound *thujone*, thought to have been the culprit in absinthe.

Today absinthe is once again produced by hundreds of companies following modern food and beverage laws. In France, the French Absinthe Ban of 1915 was repealed in 2011, causing an upsurge of interest in it as a botanical-based spirit. The most typical ingredients include grande wormwood, green anise, Florence fennel, angelica, and star anise.

The French method for serving it involves a ritual of placing a sugar cube on the top of an absinthe spoon, which has decorative holes so that when the spoon is placed over a glass of absinthe, water poured over the sugar cube will drop into the glass and turn the absinthe below into a cloudy white mixture. Vintage absinthe glasses, fountains, and silver spoons have also come into demand.

SWEET SWISS CHARD TART
La Tourte de Blettes Sucrée

Of all the foods typical to Nice, this sweet tart has to be one of the most iconic. At the open-air market in Nice or in old town, there is bound to be someone selling a freshly made sweet *tourte de blette*, a pie filled with Swiss chard, onions, rum-soaked raisins, apple, pear, and pine nuts, and often frosted with confectioners' sugar. Some recipes call for orange flower water. Some use blond raisins that have soaked in rum for half a day. One baker in old town makes his with crystallized melons and oranges. There is a savory version as well.

I like to incorporate some chopped crystalized fruit in mine. It may be hard to find candied fruit except around the holidays, although health food stores and gourmet shops usually have candied slices of papaya, pineapple, and apple, which you can chop up and add to this recipe.

Serves 8

5 tablespoons raisins

2 ounces dark rum

2 pounds Swiss chard

3 tablespoons dark brown sugar

1/2 cup finely chopped candied fruit

1/2 cup chopped walnuts

2 eggs, beaten

1 tablespoon olive oil

   dash of salt

   zest of 1/2 organic orange

2 piecrusts (recipe on page 177)

1 apple, 1/4-inch slices

1 pear, 1/4-inch slices

1 tablespoon granulated sugar

Preheat the oven to 375 degrees F. Spray a 10-inch springform pan with olive oil.

Soak the raisins in rum for 30 minutes.

Remove stalks from the Swiss chard and wash the leaves. Dry on paper towels. Roll and slice the leaves into 1/4-inch strips. You should have about 4 tightly packed cups of chard leaves. (Use the stalks for a soup or salad.) Set aside.

In a large bowl, put the raisins, rum, brown sugar, candied fruit, walnuts, eggs, olive oil, salt, and orange zest; mix well. Add the Swiss chard and mix again.

Press one of the piecrusts into the bottom of the springform pan, pressing some up the sides. Top with the chard mixture and press down with a spatula. Alternate slices of apple and pear in circles to cover the top of the Swiss chard mixture. Sprinkle 1 tablespoon sugar over the top of the fruit, then top with the second piecrust.

Sprinkle with sugar, prick several times with a fork, and bake for 35 minutes. Allow to cool before removing from the springform pan.

TASTING PLATE: CANDIED ORANGE PEEL, CHOCOLATE MARZIPAN ROCKS, FRESH CHESTNUT CANDIES

Degustation: Les Écorces D'Oranges Confites, Les Bonbons de Chocolat et Massepain, Les Bonbons de Châtaignes Fraîches

When I juice citrus fruit for recipes or for making cocktails, rather than throw away the rinds, I make homemade candied rind. It takes little effort and the result is sublime. The first few are eaten right away; some are served that night for dessert, and a couple end up wedged onto an espresso cup. The next morning, they're most likely chopped and mixed into orange marmalade for breakfast. Suddenly, there are none left.

Candied rinds have become one of my go-to desserts when company is coming. Combining them with chocolates on a large tasting plate is always a hit when served with espresso and brandy or a fine liqueur.

For this tasting plate, I've included candied orange rind, dark chocolate rocks filled with marzipan, and fresh chestnut candies.

Make the candied orange rinds and chestnut candies the day before you would like to serve them; the chocolate rocks can be made the same day.

Serves 4-6

FOR THE CANDIED ORANGE PEEL

Makes about 40 pieces

- 4 organic non-waxed oranges, washed
- 2 cups sugar, plus more for dredging
- 4 tablespoons orange flower water, optional

FOR THE CHOCOLATE ROCKS

Makes 20 pieces

- 6 ounces semisweet dark chocolate, finely chopped
- 1 tablespoon unsalted butter
- 1 teaspoon instant espresso coffee powder, optional
- 2 (2.5-ounce) packages almond slivers
- 1 small can or package marzipan

FOR THE CHESTNUT CANDIES

- 2 cups chestnuts, fresh roasted and peeled or from a jar
- 3 cups sugar
- 1 cup water
- 1 star anise, broken

Slice the oranges in half, juice them, and enjoy the juice! Slice the rinds in half again to quarter. With a serrated knife, slice away the remaining pulp, leaving a fat cushion of pith but skimming off a little bit of the pith nearest the pulp.

Slice the peel in 1/4-inch to 1/2-inch-wide strips. Place in a pot with enough cold water to cover the peels by 1 inch; bring to a boil and then drain into a colander. Put the peels back into the pot and fill with fresh cold water to cover by 1 inch. Continue as before, repeating this blanching process 4 more times, for a total of 5 times, to eliminate any bitterness in the peels.

After the fifth blanching, return the peels to the pot, add 2 cups sugar and enough water to cover the peels by 1 inch; bring to a boil, turn down to a low heat, and cook until the peels have become translucent, 45 minutes or longer. Be careful not to touch the hot syrup at any point in the process, and resist stirring, as it might cause the sugar to crystalize.

Remove from the heat and allow to cool to room temperature; then cover and refrigerate overnight.

The next morning, lay a large piece of parchment paper on a work surface. Pour some sugar in a large tray or dish. With a fork, remove the peels from the syrup and lay them in the sugar, tossing them and using your fingertips to gently press them down in the sugar so it adheres to all sides. Move the sugar-coated peels to the parchment paper and allow to dry for at least 3 hours.

To make the chocolate rocks, melt the chocolate, butter, and optional espresso powder in a double boiler or heat-proof bowl over a pot of simmering water. Stir to blend, and when completely melted, gently stir in the slivered almonds. Remove from the heat and continue to stir until the mixture is cool enough to handle and shape.

Lay out a large piece of parchment paper on a baking tray. Take a small piece of marzipan and roll it into a ball. With a teaspoon, scoop some of the chocolate mixture, top it with the ball of marzipan, and cover with another teaspoon of chocolate. Use your hands to cover the marzipan completely with the chocolate to make a ball shape. Place on the parchment paper and continue until all the chocolate is used. Place the tray of chocolate rocks in the refrigerator for at least 30 minutes.

To make the chestnut candies, slice the chestnuts into quarters.

Place a large piece of parchment paper on the counter or a baking pan.

In a saucepan, stir sugar and water till dissolved. Add star anise. On medium heat, bring the mixture to a boil; continue cooking until the temperature reaches 240 degrees F. on a candy thermometer. Remove from the heat and stir in the chestnuts until it looks milky.

Pour the mixture onto the parchment paper, using a fork to separate the chestnuts (or mass them into clusters). Make sure to locate the star anise and discard. Allow to dry.

To make the tasting plate, arrange three bowls, each one filled with one of the above confections, on a rectangular or serving platter.

*Note: Adding the orange flower water to the pot adds a lovely extra layer of orange flavor and aroma to the peels. Other additions at this point could include a cinnamon stick, star anise, lavender, or Grand Marnier.

FÊTE DES ORANGES, BAR-SUR-LOUP

How could I not make candied orange peels during the orange festival in my village? Every year, Bar-sur-Loup holds a festival in honor of the bigarade bitter orange. It's held on Easter Monday with a concert and animated fireworks set to music, as well as traditional folkloric dancers in costume, tapping their way up and down the streets. This little town really loves to dance!

There are exhibitions about our oranges, and a market where bitter orange marmalade and orange wine and liqueur made in the village are sold.

Acknowledgments

As the result of culinary mentors who were either neighbors or friends; a father and grandmother who shared with me their love for cooking and dining; thousands of meals from which I scribbled down notes and impressions; literally hundreds of cookbooks I have read and devoured; I am indebted to almost every restaurant, meal, fruit vendor, butcher, friend, chef, and book I have ever interacted with. As a culmination of that knowledge, I cook.

Huge thank-yous and hugs go to all the home cooks and chefs along the Côte d'Azur who shared their recipes with me and helped me learn more about cuisine Niçoise. You were my guides.

Heartfelt thanks, as well, to the talented chefs who created recipes to contribute to this book: Nicolas Rondelli, chef at Le Bigaradier at L'Hostellerie du Château in Bar-sur-Loup; Sébastien Broda, chef at Le Park45 at Le Grand Hotel in Cannes; and Pascal Bardet, chef at La Passagère at Hôtel Belles Rives in Juan-les-Pins. And to Stephan Smith, personal chef and friend, my thanks.

So many people who follow my blogs stepped forward to volunteer to test recipes for this book; I want to thank each of you. For those who went above and beyond, testing recipe after recipe, over and over, I wish to especially thank the intrepid Carl di Prima, Sandy Gerlach Sidwell, Barbara Michelson, Jennifer Cartmel, and Susan Laughlin.

Steven Rothfeld, the brilliant genius behind the photography for this cookbook, provided me with stunningly beautiful visual depictions of the food I love to make as well as with his warmth, favorite music, and friendship. We are equal partners in this opus.

Deborah Ritchken, my extraordinary agent, you are every writer's dream. Cheerleader, divine food stylist, witty and wise companion, and unfailing fellow Francophile, I can't imagine better. Thank you, Deborah.

This book would not have been possible without the encouragement and support of my treasured friends, Kenneth Sheptoff, Joanie and Jeremy Frost, Sandy Taylor for her insightful counsel and early editing, Blandine Beaulieu, George Sheinberg, Heather Pilley, Foster Thalheimer, Barbara Michelson, Marie-France Mathes, and Susan Laughlin, as well as my former husband for joining me on one of life's great adventures and for providing fun and support along the way.

I loved working with my editor, Madge Baird, who gave me so much encouragement and freedom to write my stories and to contribute my ideas to the production of the book. She was eminently easy to work with, and this book would not have been possible without her. My thanks as well to the entire team at Gibbs Smith for your invaluable input in creating such a beautiful design. Thank you for all that you do.

And to all the people who provided me with support in France—Homeaway.com and Jaime Dito, AutoEurope.com and Nanci Sullivan, and to the formidable people connector Janine Seulmaison—thank you all.

Last but not least, I want to thank all of the people who I interact with every day on my blogs, twitter, Facebook, Youtube and Pinterest. Your enthusiasm, friendship, loyalty, and counsel are greatly appreciated.

Index

METRIC CONVERSION CHART

VOLUME MEASUREMENTS		WEIGHT MEASUREMENTS		TEMPERATURE CONVERSION	
U.S.	Metric	U.S.	Metric	Fahrenheit	Celsius
1 teaspoon	5 ml	1/2 ounce	15 g	250	120
1 tablespoon	15 ml	1 ounce	30 g	300	150
1/4 cup	60 ml	3 ounces	90 g	325	160
1/3 cup	75 ml	4 ounces	115 g	350	180
1/2 cup	125 ml	8 ounces	225 g	375	190
2/3 cup	150 ml	12 ounces	350 g	400	200
3/4 cup	175 ml	1 pound	450 g	425	220
1 cup	250 ml	2 1/4 pounds	1 kg	450	230